rock|fashion

joshua sims

OMNIBUS PRESS

Text by Joshua Sims

Edited by Mal Peachey

Design by Pearce Marchbank, Ben May/Studio Twenty

Picture research by Nikki Russell and Sean Delany

Text layout by Ben May, Phil Levene

Contributors

Tom Gilbey is a Savile Row tailor and style guru to many.
He makes great waistcoats.
Nik Cohn is a very famous and stylish writer.
He wrote, among other things, *Saturday Night Fever*.
Michael Fish is one of the best shirtmakers ever.
He owned the Mr Fish boutique (London & NY).
Simon Jordan works at Magic Hat.
They tell companies what the kids want, and why.
Andrew Loog Oldham left school at 16 and discovered The
Rolling Stones. He lives in Bogota.
Tony Calder, a consumate music man , was a founding figure in
Immediate Records.
Jack Good was one of Britain's first and greatest music TV producers.
He now lives in the desert.
Christopher Gibbs was Britain's first rock 'n' roll Dandy.
He is a delaler in fine antiques.
Nick Logan left the editor's chair at *NME* and started *The Face*
and then *Arena* magazines.
Paul Smith is one of the internationally best known clothes designers
Britain has produced.
Tommy Hilfiger is *that* Tommy Hilfiger.
Mary Quant is the one and only Mary Quant.
Vivienne Westwood invented the punk look in 1976.
She still makes great, shocking outfits.

Writer's acknowledgments

Big thanks go to all those who have contributed their experiences, knowledge and insight
to this book, the old hands and the young guns. Also to the players at Essential Books:
Emma Dickens for her post-it notes and perseverance, John Conway for his calm
presence and Mal Peachey for his insistence that rock fashion didn't begin in the
Seventies. For foot-tappers and dedicated followers everywhere.

Bibliography

Wham Bam Thank You Glam *Novick/Middles – Aurum Press*
MTV-Cyclopedia *Duerden – Sevenoaks*
The Rolling Stones, A Life on the Road *Lowenstein/Holland – Virgin*
Subculture: The Meaning of Style *Hebdige – Routledge*
Today There Are No Gentlemen *Cohn – Weidenfeld & Nicolson*
Revolt Into Style *Melly – Penguin*
Empire Made *Rawlings/Badman – Complete Music*
Essential Elvis *Silverton – Chameleon*
Elvis in the Beginning *Wertheimer – Pimlico*
Haircults *Jones – Thames & Hudson*
The Black Leather Jacket *Farren – Abbeville*
Yesterday *Freeman – Holt*
The Moment *Furmanovsky – Paper Tiger*
Totally Awesome Eighties *Rettenmund – St Martins Griffin*
Unknown Pleasures *Stump – Quartet*
Fashion and Perversity *Vermorel – Bloomsbury*
The Best Years of The Beatles *Best/Harry – Headline*
Vested Interests *Garber –id Penguin*

Exclusive distributors
Book Sales Limited,
8-9 Frith Street,
London W1V 5TZ, UK.
Music Sales Corporation,
257 Park Avenue South,
New York, NY 10010, USA.
The Five Mile Press,
22 Summit Road, Noble Park,
Victoria 3174, Australia.

To the Music Trade only
Music Sales Limited,
8-9 Frith Street,
London W1V 5TZ, UK.

ISBN 0.7119.7733
Order No: OP 48155

Picture credits

Front cover picture: Gamma Press/Frank Spooner Pictures; Richie Aaron/Redferns: 14tl;
Eugene Adebari/Rex: 11tr, 60b, 99, 130tc, 213br, 215bl, 223bl; Advertising Archives:
11b, 96r, 102, 159b, 162t, 195l & tr, 215br; Glen A.Baker/Redferns: 180cl; Barnaby's:
27, 55, 66b, 85cr, 123r, 170b, 171cl, 220tl; Dick Barnatt/Redferns: 112t; Michael
Benabib/Retna: 41br, 223t; Adrian Boot/Retna: 88r, 160br; Andy Booth/Redferns: 209c;
Camera Press: 114bl; Brian Cooke: 14b; Corbis: 88l, 167r, 199b; Corbis-Bettmann/UPI:
18, 67, 73b, 90, 111b, 116t, 156br, 164, 216, 220br; David Corio/Retna: 41c;
Fin Costello/ Redferns; 97b, 119tl, 161t; Ian Dickson/Redferns: 136r; Henry Diltz/
Corbis: 76l; Kieran Doherty/Redferns:19t; Steve Double/SIN: 135l;
Lynn Goldsmith/Corbis: 36l, 52, 57tr, 180b; Martin Goodacre/Retna: 204cl;
Harry Goodwin: 31b, 53b, 105br, 168, 172t & b, 173, 187t, 189tl, 192, 193, 194bl & tr,
205t; Ronald Grant Archive: 19b; Dezo Hoffman/Rex: 21b, 28b, 53t, 114t, 212t;
DaveHogan/Rex: 103, 139t, 209t, 214; Mick Hutson/Redferns: 53c;
Warren Johnson/Rex: 139tc; Nils Jorgenson/Rex: 181; Astrid Kirchherr/Redferns: 8t,
24tl, 171b; Kobal Collection: 6b; Elliott Landy/Redferns: 113b; Youri Lenquette/ Retna:
105c, 139b, 184tc; LFI: cover insets, 7t, 13b, 14tr, 15b, 17b, 20, 21t, 24bl, 25b, 34, 36b,
37, 41t, 42/43, 45l, 46t, 48t, 49b, 50t, 56br, 57b, 59b, 64r, 66t, 70, 72, 73t, 81b, 85br,
87b, 91, 96t, 97t, 98, 101tr, 110tr, 120l & b, 121, 125l, 129l & c, 131tl & c, 134, 140t & b,
141, 143, 144, 145, 152b, 156bl, 172bl, 174, 175l & r, 179b, t & cr, 180tl, 183t, 184tl & b,
187b & tr, 189t & r, 194tl & br, 196tr, 197, 198, 201t, 202/203, 204t, br & c, 205b, 206,
207, 208, 209b, 213bl, 219, 222r; Gerard Malanga: 79, 210/211; Mirror Syndication Int:
12tr, 117; Keith Morris/Redferns: 212b; Michael Ochs Archive/Redferns: 6tl, 13cr, 30,
45r, 74, 151l, 152t, 166t, 169; Mark C.O'Flaherty: 124b, 147; Dennis O'Regan/Corbis:
56t; Ernie Paniccioli/Retna: 139b; Photofest: 7b, 217t; Pictorial Press: cover insets, 4r,
9t, 10, 11tl, 12c, 24cr, 28t, 32tl, 33, 35tl & c, 48b, 49t, 51tr, 60tl & r, 61, 62, 64bl, 66c,
76b, 80, 81tr, 82/3, 85l, 96l&b, 104l & r, 105t, 106l, 108, 109b, 110tl & b, 112t & br, 120tr,
124t, 129r, 130b, 146l & r, 154/155, 156l, 158, 163, 170tl & r, 171tl & r, 172cr, 175t & b,
176, 177, 178, 179cl, 180cr, 183l, 189tr & b, 191, 200t, 201b, 213tr, 215tl & r;
Barry Plummer: 135r; Dick Polak: 15c, 56bl, 81tl, 85tr, 162bl, 213tl; Popperfoto: 22t, 59l,
115, 137; Steve Pyke/Retna: 204bl; Neal Preston/Retna: 183r; Brian Rasic/Rex: 5;
David Redfern: 119tr; Redferns: 31t; Retna: 58,139bc, 152l, 218r, 223br;
Rex: cover insets, 4l, 8b, 9b, 16, 17tr, 23, 24br, 25t, 26, 29, 32tr & b, 35cr, 46b, 47, 50b,
53t, 54, 56bc, 57tl & c, 63, 64tl, 65, 75, 86t, 92, 93, 94/5, 101l & b, 104c, 105bl, 106r,
111t, 112bl, 116b, 119b, 120t, 122, 123b, 125r, 126, 127, 128l, 130tl & r, 131tr & b,
132/133, 152r, 153, 156t, 159tr, 160t & bl, 161, 162br, 165r, 170c, 179tl, 180tr, 182,
184cl, 186, 187l, 188, 195br, 202bl, 218l, 222l, 224l&r; DerekRidgers/ Barnaby's: 157, 185;
Mick Rock/Star File: 201r; Sheila Rock/Rex: 86b, 89, 200bl; Ebet Roberts/Redferns:
35br; Roger Sargent/Rex: 36tr, 190; S&G/Redferns: 136l; Kate Simon: 109t;
Paul Slattery/Retna: 220bl, 221; Sotheby's: 40, 44, 68, 69, 71; Ray Stevenson/Rex: 87t,
199t; Superstock: 41bl; Stephen Sweet/Rex: 138; Nick Tansley/All Action: 107, 148,
149; John Tiberi/Redferns: 59r; Ian T.Tilton/Retna: 100; Julian Wasser/SIN: 77, 114br,
118, 159tl & cr; Scott Weiner/Retna: 202tl; Richard Young/Rex: 35tr, 38/39, 51b, 67, 78,
123t, 142, 179tr, 200br.

rock|fashion

Liam Gallagher, frontman of Oasis in a parka, 1997. The bag could be 1964

Liam Gallagher, front-man for Oasis, probably the biggest UK band of the Nineties and therefore one of the top Faces of the decade, wore a parka in a video for their 'Do Y'Know What I Mean'. The parka has no role in the song, or its video, or the story which either tells. Gallagher (or his stylist), it seems, simply decided he would wear a parka in this video, perhaps as a nod to the Mod movement, fashionable at the time and to which the members of Oasis had some natural affiliation. The following day, a cutting-edge clothes store in London – the one rumoured to have been where Gallagher bought his parka – sold out its remaining stock. Army surplus stores, re-established as a favourite fashion haunt for combat trousers among the trend-setters of the Nineties, were inundated with people looking for parkas. By the next autumn/winter fashion season, even big name designers, notably Helmut Lang, were offering parkas. Thus one rock star, in one video, helped dress the nation to resemble extras from the film version of The Who's early Seventies paean to Mod, *Quadrophenia*.

This story reflects a new relationship between rock star and pop consumer, a symbiotic one. Once fans wanted their rock stars to be different, to indicate some point of departure from the norm, to rock the boat with the way they dressed as much as the music they played, super-beings to whom a fan might pay homage by wearing a similar jacket or the same type of eye-shadow. Now star and fan wear the very same jacket. The fan might even have been wearing it before the rock star. Because it's not just the rock star that has changed and become less theatrical, more mundane, more of

Stylist-dressed first generation Mod showband, The Who

Facing page: Lauryn Hill, queen of hip-hop in designer leather

the people in the last decade of the twentieth century: It's the fan too. They are more sceptical, more media and marketing-literate, aware of the manoeuvrings behind stage by a team of stylists who get the stars' clothes for free, who pick outfits that express less the star than the product the fan can buy into. The fan is always suspicious that he or she is being sold to.

At the end of the Nineties, rock star and fan alike come from the same culture. The rock star reflects in his dress the culture he was naturally part of before becoming famous. Fans, too, may have been part of that culture and dress alike. What the rock star does now to influence fashion is to introduce a

Tommy Hilfiger
puffa top

particular look to a wider audience – in marketing parlance, to push the product or brand beyond the early aficionados to a mass customer base. Rock star and fan have become one, a yin and yang mutually influenced and influential.

Not that marketing has killed all the mystique. It might be getting that way by turning rock fashion into an exercise in branding, certainly. But rock stars still hold an all-important allure. Both from the marketing directors' bottom-line point of view, and the fans' often still willingly mythologising one, the rock star can make or break a look. It is now established thinking in marketing circles that the best way to create a volume product is to get it used by trend-setters. The rest will happen naturally, filtering down through the fashion food chain. But there has to be some authenticity in the connection between band and product. US fashion giant Tommy Hilfiger, for instance, asked a marketing guru and scene-maker to identify a rising star for him to approach to wear Hilfiger gear. Puff Daddy, having only recently made his breakthrough at the time, was selected. Puff wore Tommy's undies. Next day, the world's populace (fashion information

A young Elvis in lipstick and eyeliner, nicely offset by the tweed lounge jacket

being transmitted almost instantaneously via global media) was buying Tommy Hilfiger underwear. But Puff and his fans knew that the brand was already being worn by their more low-key peers. Puff simply gave it a more public seal of approval. No matter what they offered, Marks & Spencer could not have struck the same deal.

Similarly, US rap group Run DMC's song 'My adidas' was ostensibly about how the adidas shell-toe trainer became associated with gangsters (largely, the story goes, because over-production led adidas to sell a job-lot to the US penitentiary service, resulting in new ex-cons hitting the streets in shell-toes). When the song was released, the product was already an established part of Run DMC's culture. They were wearing it anyway. But it helped put adidas on the map in fashion terms. Would they have worn the product if adidas had approached the band and it wasn't already part of the culture? It's doubtful.

The relationship between rock star, fashion and fan is as complex as relationships driven by marketing can be. The marketing departments behind most bands also realise that while a point of difference is welcome and that star quality can still come in the shape of a well-cut suit or a giant cut

"It wasn't until Bill Haley came to Britain that Teddy Boys became the archetypal ruffian. Before that it had been about posing, but the music gave people a reason to dress up other than to parade around looking in shop windows at yourself."

Tom Gilbey

Bill Hayley and his Comets rock around the clock in Hawaian leisure wear

Before Epstein: Hamburg-era, Gene Vincent-inspired Beatles with drummer Pete Best (left) and Stuart Sutcliffe (right)

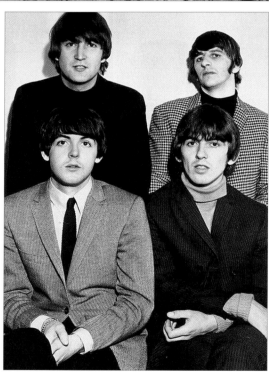

After Epstein: Boys next door-era Beatles

diamond ring, stars have to be obtainable. A point of identification with the star is needed, rather than a mysterious and exciting alienation. Emulation has to be possible. Fans still look to rock stars for fashion guidance. Rock stars, for all the cynicism that surrounds them, remain trend-setters almost by default.

Before Epstein: Hamburg-era, Gene Vincent-inspired Beatles with drummer Pete Best (left) and Stuart Sutcliffe (right)

It hasn't always been this way, however. Once, rock stars were the untouchables, on a pedestal as much for their preening and the cut of their cloth as for their excessive lifestyles. Whatever happened to the snake-skin suit? The outrageous glitter? The too-cool shades? The skin-tight black jackets and countless rings (worn over leather gloves, naturally)? These were the true motifs of rock-stardom that an adoring public would tentatively try to copy, invariably making a real hash of it. These motifs were as much a part of a rock star's persona as the music. Ridiculous to modern tastes many of them may well have been, but without them, Elton John was just plain Reg Dwight, Gary Glitter only Paul Gadd, Alice Cooper plain old Vincent Furnier. Now, Robbie Williams is Robbie Williams. And he dresses like a Robbie Williams. Everybody dresses like Robbie Williams.

There were more than three decades that typified the very best of rock fashion, a period when rock's relationship with fashion was in part a story of how it overturned conventions and forced a reappraisal of the meaning of clothing. One could even say that pre-rock 'n' roll, dress was used,

The Beatles try out evening wear circa 1963

then as now, as a complex code of social identification, to create a sense of propriety or belonging. Suits and dresses were conventional and early rock stars, the crooners and the family entertainers, wore suits and dresses that were much the same suits and dresses worn in much the same way as their audience. There was no marketing plan in this. Every man wore a suit. Every woman wore a dress. End of story. After Elvis turned up with his collar and his trousers swayed, fashion was never the same.

From the Fifties and Elvis, through to the Seventies and Sly Stone, rock and fashion lived happily side by side, without ever getting serious about each other. Of course, rock bands and their management were always aware of what would and wouldn't help to shift records other than putting out good songs. The Beatles' radical overhaul from greased-up rockers to floppy-fringed boys-next-door in their neat suits is a classic example of a svengali make-over. Bands often dressed seemingly counter to the stereotypical dress for their music in order to tap into a fashion theme of the day and boost their credibility, or find a new audience. Often, especially in Britain, they used the very best avant-garde designers of the day to create a look for them. Unlike the brandcentric approach of today, the designers went largely unsung, which meant that lads had to go to their local tailors with a newspaper cutting and ask for 'Something like that', rather than go to the local mall and buy the self-same logoed garment. Some of these designers are rightly celebrated in this book.

The advent of TV encouraged rock music's love of denim, leather, white T-shirts, short skirts, men in dresses, women in trousers, dye, pan-cake and glitter. A rock star was defined by the manner in which their appearance differed from the norm: Elvis, Little Richard, Ronnie Spector, David Bowie, Debbie Harry, Siouxsie Sioux, Jim Morrison, James Brown, The Sex Pistols, Kurt Cobain, and so on. Fashion helped rock stars define their rebellion, revolution, teen angst, sex and theatricality, and thus helped define it for their fans. Rock stars learned the benefit of teasing and shocking, of making a visual as well as an aural impact. These were years when rock star dress could cause a riot, could crumple the very social fabric.

In many instances, a certain style of dress came to be a visual trademark for the performer, not necessarily one that had an impact on the wider fashion scene, but nevertheless one that became almost as central to that stars' success as the music. If rock stars have helped define a generation with their dress, then their dress has also helped define that star to that generation. Certain clothes, looks or accessories became so tightly bound-up with their originators (at

Punk's first sex kitten, Debbie Harry of Blondie

"Once Bryan Ferry and Bowie would set the fashion tone and that's what the audience wanted them to do. Now rock fans want something they can identify with. The fashion look has to be obtainable."

Simon Jordan of Magic Hat

"David Bowie. He used to come in the shop with his wife. To see him working on what he wanted and coming up with things like wearing that Panne velvet which was actually Yves Saint Laurent. To have a feeling for a look as much as he had and then to go on to work with Yamamoto is a great turn. And what's more he appreciates it, gives credit for it, he doesn't say 'just another outfit'. Indeed at one point I think clothes were more important to him than the music."

Michael Fish

Thin White Duke era Bowie

least in the public imagination) that it was almost impossible to separate them. Thick-rimmed glasses? Buddy Holly. Leather jacket? Gene Vincent. Snakeskin trousers? Jim Morrison. Zips? Johnny Rotten. The brighter rock acts of the past few decades realised this: they were either originals in the first place, wearing an original look, or they found originality fast, be it in a key detail such as Michael Jackson's perennial white socks (which were transformed into the logo for his company, Michael Jackson Productions), Sandy Shaw's bare feet or Bryan Ferry's white tuxedo.

This last example best illustrates the close relationships that have formed between certain designers and performers. As with Madonna and Jean-Paul Gaultier, Anthony Price's association with Ferry was widely recognised in the Seventies and early Eighties, tying the two worlds. The wider, somehow more decadent white-jacket dinner suits designed by Price for Ferry defined the singer's image as an arch smoothie, suggestive of refinement, taste, privilege, luxury and Bondian sexual aggression all at once; as well as, Ferry has noted, harking back to the balladeering crooners of Sinatra's time. Given Ferry's art school background, it could even have been described as a pop art comment on the superficiality of glamour (as explored by the pop group and club-driven New Romantic movement of the early Eighties).

Such was Ferry's insistence on staying true to the fashion image created for him that when performing in Scotland he even wore his tux over a kilt. Price, whose King's Road shop Plaza also supplied the clothes for the mannequins on the cover of Roxy Music's *Manifesto* LP, has put it more

The Rolling Stones on the cover of the 5x5 EP. Individual style as opposed to The Beatles' homogeneity

Bowie in the Michael Fish man's 'dress' that almost got him shot in Texas

directly: "The white tuxedo… will be the image on his gravestone." Similarly, Boy George, a performer who always claimed he wore not dresses but robes like a bishop or priest, going as far as to appear in a nun's habit for one early performance, was so closely tied by association with the androgynous look that he followed up fan interest by publishing a book of clothing patterns, together with make-up instructions.

Indeed, rock stars of all music types, among them Bowie, The New York Dolls, Siouxsie Sioux and Kurt Cobain, have not missed a beat in recognising the shock value, perhaps even the artistic value, of challenging stereotype through cross-dressing. Both women dressing as men (Annie Lennox, Madonna, Grace Jones), and more commonly men dressing as women, offer the most striking examples of how rock stars have subverted the conformist nature of dress. Grace Jones in particular popularised the suit as a form of dress for the female public. Whether these rock star antics had an impact on their public that lasted, even despite the huge publicity surrounding them and the power of their own media, is debatable. Initially, it may have literally rocked the boat. But, as the few members of society for whom cross-dressing was socially acceptable, it became less an art statement by rock stars than almost expected, a cliché of outrageous rock 'n' roll behaviour. So blasé did the fans

Brian Jones, the Stones' fashion leader

become about this tactic that, come a 1984 reader poll, Dee Snider, frontman of Twisted Sister, was voted one of the worst-dressed women of the year. Similarly, in the same year, Annie Lennox, well-known for her gender-bending cropped and coloured hair, made an appearance at the Grammy Awards in full Elvis drag. This anything-goes approach was one distinct way in which rock and fashion became inextricably linked.

Make-up, too, was toyed with, producing similar results, emulated only by those record-buyers who were into New Romanticism in the Eighties: a movement which gave the public Spandau Ballet and a love affair with the flouncy shirt. From the ladies of the Sixties who invented glam, such as Diana Ross in her false eyelashes and Marianne Faithfull with her more alternative white lipstick, to the men, make-up belonged on the rock star's stage. Since the late Fifties at least, rockers have seen cosmetics as part of their paraphernalia. Even Elvis, who came to personify masculine sexuality, wore so much eyeliner in his early career that Chet Atkins commented that "It was like seeing a couple of guys kissing in Key West." As Liberace, the flamboyant singer and dresser who prefigured the likes of Grace Jones, Jackson and others by dressing in capes and epaulettes, once commented, "Now it's not unusual for one male rocker to say to another, 'May I borrow your eyeliner?' And practically no man is above borrowing his best friend's skin bronzer."

Elvis and Liberace were aware of the need for rock stars and performers to dress apart from the fans and, in doing so, challenge and change society's norms. Liberace described his offstage clothes as straight. And, he added, "Elvis and I may be characters, me with my gold jackets and him with his sideburns, but we can afford to be."

Indeed, rock stars were expected to be. The need to keep topping both each other and in some instances their own previous efforts, began with the gold lamé suit Elvis appropriated from

Flash trash glam shoes with ankle-snapping five-inch heels

Liberace's style notebook, and culminated in the Bill Belew-designed, camp, if not feminised, jewelled white leather jump-suits, pearls and furs he ended up in during the early Seventies – and the dress excess that was glam. Just as this jumpsuited image of Elvis unfortunately became the one seemingly set in the public imagination, glam's excesses caught the eye, but seemed unlikely to find a high street equivalent. Yet it did. And not just with the kids. Grown-ups saw David Johansen and went on to wear spangly flares, stack heels and big hats. They grew their hair, grew sideburns, grew to look very silly indeed. Perhaps this was the moment when the future merger of public and rock star was set in motion.

The Ronettes; Beehive hair, mascara'd eyes and pouting lips circa 1964

Until the early Nineties, when this truly became the case, rock stars knew a look was essential. It provided a way around social barriers: the wild costumes of Little Richard's early career – the blouses, the capes and the outrageous conk hairdo – were, he said, a way of overcoming racial constraints. "We decided that my image should be crazy and way-out so that the adults would think I was harmless. I'd appear in one show dressed as the Queen of England, and in the other dressed as the Pope…" But it also attempted to break down these barriers. Put Elvis in a dark suit, loose tie and fedora and he wouldn't have become Frank Sinatra – the essence of urbane cool though Frank was. He would have become square and unthreatening. Elvis had to look different to work. Forty years later, The Prodigy would try to shock an almost unshockable public with multiple-piercing, a new take on punk haircuts and fright-night contact lenses. But for the times, Elvis went further. He sang with a black voice. He was a white Southern boy who sang black music. He had to dress like a black ghetto boy, a white dude in aliens clothes – let's try a pink suit, let's try turning up the collar – to hit the mark. And, having grown up in a neighbourhood so poor it was full of black folk, that's what he'd been wearing since school.

The Ronettes: inventing sex

Elvis became the first rock star in embryo to fully understand the importance of looking unusual. Grown-ups all over the middle-west must have fainted. The kids of course, they were all right. They loved it. And while they couldn't sing like him, they could sure look like him. Elvis' hair created upheaval on the scale of a national emergency. Famously filmed on *The Ed Sullivan Show* from the

Little Richard in zoot-styled suit

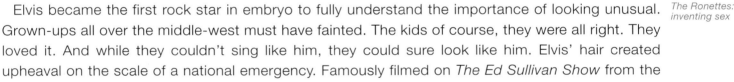

"Little Richard, that grey shot silk loose grey wonder of a suit in *The Girl Can't Help It*, all Macon Armani/ Pittsburg Paul Smith, the look is energy, svelte freedom and forever."

Andrew Loog Oldham

A different sort of evening wear; Sid Vicious in white tuxedo, Chubb lock chain and junkie tie on thigh

"I immediately thought Sid looked like a star – he had such a sullen and striking presence."

Nik Cohn

Sid in action – a pale imitation of self-mutilating Iggy Pop

waist up to avoid his jiggling hips offending family viewers, his jiggling quiff (a positive mane by Fifties standards that associated social order with the short back and sides) remained on full view. His hip gyrations were believed to offend. But it was, of course, his hair that was making all the impact. The flamboyant British Teddy Boy movement, already well-established as a counter to post-war austerity, was strong in its identity. But it wasn't strong enough to resist Elvis. His hair-style became the blueprint for the standard Ted look. It defined him to his fans just as the tux later defined Bryan Ferry. These were aspects that almost defined the performers to themselves, like character actors who switch into their new personalities when in costume. It required only the right accessory, well-used, to make an impact: Cliff Richard's white tie or Johnny Kidd's eye-patch; Larry Blackmon of Cameo's cod-piece or Madonna's conical bra (both Jean-Paul Gaultier creations).

Such has been the importance of the rock fashion wardrobe that the clothes the stars wore often came to overshadow the rock stars themselves. They had a significance and a cultural influence beyond the stars themselves, influencing the way fashion moved, the way different cultural groups were shaped and how they prospered. For every Rolling Stone tune immortalised there has been an MC Hammer fashion horror engraved on the public consciousness. His raps may be forgotten, but his gigantic trousers live on in memories of that early Eighties era. 'Can't Touch This', he sang, and he

Spandau Ballet's Martin Kemp didn't need no pressure on. Should have dressed a bit more sensibly, then

was right. In those pants you wouldn't even be able to find it.

But while the MC Hammer look, as well as the more stagey, and more memorable, rock star outfits of the past forty years, didn't exactly become mainstream fashion, many other rock fashion trends did: Beatle haircuts, Michael Jackson's glove, Beastie Boys' VW insignia, Blondie's peroxide, The Who's target tops, Lou Reed's heroin chic, Kraftwerk's mannequin exactness, Adam Ant's pirate, Spandau Ballet's frills... Aggression moved to arrogance to camp to theatrical to the plain ridiculous and back again. Is it

any coincidence that the biggest, most memorable artists of the past forty years have also been the sharpest, most striking dressers? That when you close your eyes, you can not only hum the songs, but picture the way they looked when they first sang them? That the snappier (or weirdest) dressers were also the ones to touch a nerve, to spark off a new youth movement or revive an old one?

Were it not, for instance, for Gene Vincent's decision (or rather that of TV producer Jack Good) to abandon his blue-collar bowling shirt in favour of a style of dress much more aggressive, not only might his career have floundered along with his limp, but leather trousers, as adopted by Jim Morrison, Suzi Quatro (the first lady rocker in them), Cher *et al*, would still be the preserve of biker boys, still associated with the roar of engines rather than raw (hetero)sex. Rock's appropriation of a fashion has opened it up to the public. Similarly, although in the hands of designer Vivienne Westwood the punk dress aesthetic might well have survived for at least a season or two, without the bands to give it a grammar for its visual language, with the rock association it became a chapter in British social history, a movement that helped define a generation and a look that influences fashion over a quarter of a century later.

Indeed, in some small way all of the acts in this overview of rock fashion helped define the teenagers of their time. The language of popular music and the clothes that have gone with it were an exclusive code that kept the grown-ups out of the conversation. Sadly, it seems to have become a dead language.

The death knell to the best years of rock fashion, when rocks' stars and wild clothes were inextricably linked, when marketing stayed in the closet, had sounded by the middle of the designer decade. Bros, a teen-band phenomena

and a precursor to New Kids On The Block, Take That and Boyzone, comprised the brothers Matt and Luke Goss, together with background bassist Craig Logan, and were an almost entirely manufactured triumvirate: young, pretty, sensational. As planned, teen girls screamed and fainted.

But, in their tens of thousands, they also dressed like the band. And not in poor imitation of them, but exactly like them. The marketing minds behind Bros had deliberately set out to make this possible: the Bros uniform was inoffensively simple; leather jacket, ripped denims, Doctor Marten air-ware shoes. It stayed within the rock fashion tradition in that it was a bit quirky, a tad individualistic. People didn't normally dress like this on Britain's high streets at the end of the Eighties. At least, not for long. It was different, but it was available to anyone with a pair of scissors and a liquor store nearby. Girls shredded their Levis, bought the shoes and asked for the jacket for Christmas. The band even decorated their shoes. Not with diamonds, but with the stoppers from Grolsch beer bottles.

Or take Frankie Goes To Hollywood. Another, perhaps more flagrant, exercise in making the band accessible to consumers came in the guise of the Frankie Says T-shirt, a slogan-bearing garment modelled on Katharine Hamnett's design and borrowed by Wham! at the time of 'Wake Me Up

Before You Go-Go'. Frankie Says Relax, ran the slogan at the time of the band's breakthrough single 'Relax'. Frankie Says Peace Not War, at the time of 'Two Tribes'. T-shirt sales almost outstripped the band's record sales, and, as frontman Holly Johnson noted, every time he'd walk down the street and see someone in a Frankie Says T-shirt, he'd think, 'That's another 2p in the bank.'

Even the band dynamic was indicative of the more sweeping sartorial change to come. It had two front-men in designer gear, and three lads in jeans, T-shirts and leathers: two camp stage-players to provide the edge, three guys (collectively referred to as The Lads) with whom the lads on the street could identify. Despite Johnson's own penchant for Yohji Yamamoto suits, the T-shirt represented an access point to the band for all fans. Seen them, listened to that, bought the T-shirt.

No one but a true style rebel would even try to get away with that shirt and jacket combo. Dino at work

That commerce and rock began to weave themselves so closely together during the Eighties was perhaps no surprise. This was a decade in which the major record labels, Sony, EMI, MCA, RCA and Phonogram, began to build their empires and smaller, independent labels began to die. More multinational entertainment groups than companies concerned with publicising inspired and inspiring music, the big boys were concerned with making big bucks. They brought in the image police and the notion of making more money from merchandising opportunities than actual record sales. Rock bands became rock brands that the public could buy into. Bros and Frankie Goes To Hollywood represented perhaps the final step to the situation that typified the Nineties music scene, in which one looked at the rock star, looked at the fan, back at the rock star – and could barely tell the difference.

Such was the symbiotic relationship between rock stars and designer brands who were, by the Eighties, the driving force of fashion, rather than those unsung tailors, that the brands were being approached by the stars, all hoping that the brand's kudos would rub off on them. Whereas once a fashion designer would have killed to be worn by the right star (and there are alleged instances where designers have paid stars huge sums to wear their products), now the potentially short shelf-life of an over-exposed band, or one that acquires the wrong image by association, meant a designer with business sense had to pick his rock stars very carefully. Hip, underground brands were forced to consider the dangers of supplying the wrong artist with their product. Of course, the designer

George Michael

couldn't stop the rock star popping to a department store and buying his wares, potentially turning the most cool of labels into the most naff.

Similarly bad for rock fashion in the century's ultimate decade was the boom in dance culture, with bands who, like Underworld, Portishead, The Orb or Leftfield, revelled in the new anonymity it afforded. Those performers who equated artistry and being taken seriously with a disdain for the triviality of fashion altogether (concern about the cleanliness of one's cuffs, after all, isn't very rock 'n' roll) also signalled changes. The release of George Michael's second solo album, *Listen Without Prejudice Vol.1*, said it all: against all marketing philosophy, Michael, a man who was, throughout his career, synonymous first with a year-round tan and bouffant hair, and later with the Caesar crop and goatee beard, refused even to have his picture on the album cover.

Rock and pop music faced a necessary reappraisal of their role in the fashion world. Given the saying that there is nothing new in fashion, that all styles (however hideous) return, it would be fitting of a new millennium if the rock fraternity revived the old approach to the clothes they wear, if once again they saw it as their responsibility as rock stars to look different to their fans , and not to look like Joe Public with a model/footballer partner and a glowingly healthy bank balance; if, for instance, All

Before Elvis, there was Dino, the first King of Cool

Saints were to abandon their trainers and Top Shop attire in favour of Tina Turner's towering stilettos and chain-mail minis, if R.E.M. were to abandon their fathers of the boys-next-door look in favour of the dandy deviancy of The Kinks. In short, if they were to return to a time (one only recently past) when rock stars' dress was part of their act, when it helped define both them and fashion. When the high street followed the high priests of cool – the rock stars – and not vice versa. When ordinariness was frowned on.

Although, ironically, the relationship between rock and fashion was closer than ever by the end of the Nineties, it was a dull, unstarry kind of association. This killed a little of the magic that surrounds music. For rock music has never just been about the tunes, but about attitude; and fashion played a key role in shaping that. Without the duds, where are the dudes? All that's left is the music and, for many acts facing the new millennium, that's a dangerous path to go down. Perhaps this, ultimately, will lead to a clear-out of the charts in favour of better music, or perhaps even a return to theatricality. The rock industry is no longer dealing with those excited by MTV, but those who have absorbed it and moved on. So used to constant visual stimulation, it needs something really out there to grab its attention in the relationship of rock and fashion to come.

In the meantime, look back. To the Generation MTV reader, the thirty-plus years of down-home rock star dressing looks by turns both comic and nothing short of incendiary, but it was always eye-catching, always influential. For there was a revolution going on in Bill Hayley's kiss-curl, shaking its way through the buttered wool of Elvis' hair, deep down into the sole of a Beatle boot, across the dresses, make-up and eye-patches in David Bowie's dressing-up box. These were clothes with meaning, that signified being an outsider, as worn by outsiders. They were us-and-them clothes, widening the gap between artist and audience, defining the former, exciting the latter. As Vivienne Westwood was later to describe the spikey, studded and belligerent punk look, it was all "confrontation dressing.'

This book is a look at that confrontation.

Joshua Sims
London, March 1999

*Inoffensive Irish popsters B*Witched, 1999*

"Pop introduced the idea of the moment being all that counted. Not heritage. All was now ephemeral, including clothes."

Nik Cohn

suits

They look every inch the professional: neat, slicked-back hair, clean white shirts with black ties, chic, three-button single-breasted suits. They are at an MTV Awards ceremony, so they might well have dressed up. But this is Metallica, a band at the very extreme of ear-damage rock. And they could be your accountant. Suits are for work, weddings and funerals. They are not for rock 'n' roll. Suits are too uptight, together, tidy, not creative enough.

And yet they have had a long and distinguished career in the rock star's wardrobe. For most acts of the Fifties, the suit was what every man wore, and fledgling rock star though you may have been, that's what you wore, too. As entertainers, Jerry Lee Lewis and Sam Cooke wore dinner suits – a cabaret style echoed by the high-kicking Tom Jones – and they will long be associated with this dress. Elvis even donned serious suits for early TV appearances (including tails for one famously trite performance of 'Hound Dog').

Metallica collect their MTV Awards in Resevoir Dogs-inspired (i.e., Agnes B) black suits.

In order to play white clubs, Little Richard was also suited, but he wore a derivation of the zoot suit; baggy-trousered, pocket-chained and long-jacketed. It was a look that could have been the first genuine rock 'n' roll outfit, the first twist on the suit that could still spell trouble. Richard had seen it on the cool guys who hustled and worked the outer edges of the respectable, God-fearing society in which he grew up. Like Elvis, Richard could not fail to be impressed by the respect afforded these zoot-suited men, could not fail to be blinded by the gold and dollar green flashed by them in his poor, run-down neighbourhood. On the west coast of the USA the zoot suit had become synonymous with violence and gangsters in the late Forties when LAPD had viciously and violently put down what was

Little Richard demonstrating why The Girl Can't Help It in a zoot suit

TOM EWELL   JAYNE MANSFIELD   EDMOND O'BRIEN   CinemaScope
in THE GIRL CAN'T HELP IT

*Facing page:
On the west coast of the USA, the zoot suit had become synonymous with gangsters. Its louche style – long jackets and high-cut baggy trousers, worn with braces – was a natural for rebel rockers and imitated by the likes of 1980s bands Kid Creole And The Coconuts and Blue Rondo A La Turk*

billed as the Zoot Suit Riots – essentially little more than a racist attack on the largely Mexican zoot-suited gangs who stalked the downtown ghetto area of Watts. White society successfully emasculated the zoot suit not long after with the invention of cartoon characters the Black Crows – black birds who talked in slang and wore the wide shoulders, wide-brimmed hats and baggy trousers of the zoot and chewed cigars at of the side of their mouths. It took Little Richard's wide-eyed, wild piano thumping antics on stage and on film (*The Girl Can't Help It*, 1956) to elevate the zoot to a threatening item of clothing

Bill Hayley And The Comets get down and dirty in plaid – Hayley became a style leader for the Ted movement of the 1950s. The look mixed drainpipe trousers with the long jackets of zoot suits, adding Western bootlace ties to create an exaggerated version of Edwardianism (hence 'Teds')

Jack Good

"One of my biggest thrills was going to Cecil Gee's in Charing Cross Road and ordering bright pink, American-style suits for Lord Rockingham's XI. Even though *Oh Boy!* was in black and white, the effect on the audience in the Hackney Empire was electrifying as the curtain rose on a honking rock band dressed in those crazy pink suits. "I also fondly remember Bill Haley And The Comets appearing in London for the first time dressed in those deliciously vulgar plaid jackets. Suddenly we saw how grey London was."

once more. And for Richard it was a race thing. Fats Domino wore the innocuous uniform of all subservient black performers, the dinner suit when he pumped out his hits 'Blueberry Hill' and 'Ain't That A Shame', while Chuck Berry took a little while before adopting and adapting the British Edwardian-derived Teddy Boy suit to his stage show to duck-walk to 'Brown Eyed Handsome Man' *et al*, but Little Richard went for the threat, the danger, immediately.

In the UK, rock 'n' roll had crossed the Atlantic via the movies, primarily *Blackboard Jungle* (1955) which used Bill Haley And The Comets' 'Rock Around The Clock' on its soundtrack. Tabloid legend has it that a generation of young British men suddenly appeared at cinemas wherever the film played across Britain wearing their grandfather's old suits and, overcome by emotions that they could not control, would rip the cinema to shreds in time to Haley's exhortations. Nicknamed Teds, or Teddy Boys in reference to the cut of their Edwardian-inspired suits, recently freed from the constraints of rationing and other austere measures, these young men in their tight trousers and velvet-collared long jackets, with white shirts and often no tie at all, donned suede shoes and invented the British teenager.

In truth, the look had its origins not too far from those of the zoot suit: during the war, spivs (British wise guys) had worn velvet-collared Edwardian-cut long jackets and American sports jackets without a vent (always cut longer than the British equivalent – itself derived from the hunting jacket), over Oxford bag trousers and two-tone shoes. The Edwardian style of dress was both a class-conscious homage and snub to the ruling classes who, prior to the First World War had so lorded it over the working classes of Britain. With the end of the first World War came the beginning of the end of deference, and the middle classes began imitating the dress and habits of the upper classes without any great retribution. Hand-made Savile Row suits were always the sign of a true gentleman. The

T-Bone Walker sporting a very fine off-white Safari-style suit in Texas, late 1940s. The belt was a touch of pure showmanship

"It was really Bill Haley, Johnny Ray and Elvis that made fashion – the Teds, Rockers in drape suits with the sexuality of their tight drainpipe trousers."

Paul Smith

In the 1950s, the suit was the measure of the man. And Bill Hayley certainly measured up

Elvis in Jailhouse Rock doing wonders for unwashed, deconstructed denim trousers

"The effectiveness of a costume depends largely on what the body inside it is doing. You could dress Tina Turner in a gunny sack and she'd still look terrific on stage. But her female fans, if they copied her and wore gunny sacks, would not look terrific. They would look like what fans who try to dress like rock stars invariably are – a bunch of silly fools!

"I conclude that a costume is only as good as the performer wearing it. See Elvis (vintage 1954-59). Nobody has ever made a pair of slacks move the way he did – like sails in a hurricane. His greaser, truck-driver-looking gear complemented his music and his performance perfectly – and never competed with his face. Nor could it have possibly done. Of course, if you have a face like some notable singing knights you might want a little competition from your fancy dress."

Jack Good

vogue for a smart, non-tails style morning (or working) suit reached its stylistic pinnacle during the reign of Edward VII: it featured a thigh-length jacket with velvet collar and/or cuffs, flat-fronted trousers and doubled-breasted waistcoat worn with watch chain visible.

During the immediate post-war years, a time of great prosperity for those dealing in the black market, the spivs had their suits tailor-made, still based on the gentleman's three-piece of Edwardian times. (This look is almost perfectly captured on film by the actor George Cole as Flash Harry in the St Trinian's film series) By the mid-Fifties, the sons of the spivs and other young men who could see the appeal of the style created their own variation on the look, paying tailors to make cheaper two-piece versions of exaggerated lengths which they would then 'decorate' with their grandfather's or father's waistcoats. Coming at a time when the high street was awash in uniformity in the shape of grey,

Facing page: *Chuck Berry checking out the Mohair action*

Beatles in Gene Vincent-inspired black leather

double-breasted box-suits, the effect of the Ted look was as shocking as Elvis' wriggling pelvis had been in America.

The middle-aged Haley was something of a journeyman in his homeland. He'd played country and western and was trying some new-fangled rock 'n' roll because it seemed to be what the kids wanted. After his first tour of the UK went so well (riots, screaming girls and so on), Haley barely left. He adopted the Ted look in favour of one that had previously been based on the uniform of Texan swing bands crossed with standard evening wear, retaining the bootlace tie which in turn was picked up by the British Teds. Later in Chuck Berry's career, when a British rock 'n' roll revival was well under way and The Rolling Stones were championing Berry, he, too, fully embraced the Ted look.

During the Fifties, Elvis' suits were mostly of American derivation, being (usually) black and two-piece with pleated trouser fronts and three-button single-breasted fastening jacket worn with collar and lapels turned up. On the whole, though, he preferred separates, donning Dino-inspired sports jackets and loose, pleated trousers. Later, Elvis would wear a prison suit to great effect in *Jailhouse Rock*, a gold dinner suit for the famous cover of *6,000,000 Elvis Fans Can't Be Wrong*, and a black leather suit for his 1968 *Comeback Special*, before relaxing into his overstuffed, rhinestone encrusted romper suits until falling off his toilet seat dead.

The Beatles really made the suit an essential part of the rock wardrobe. Or, more specifically, Brian Epstein did. Until the management came on the scene, The Beatles were image-conscious but essentially quiff and biker boys, or a motley mix of lilac jackets, worn with black shirts with a silver stripe on the collar – as one Mersey Beat columnist put it, 'unmindful of uniformity of dress, unkempt like long hair'. Epstein realised the necessity of broadening the group's appeal, boosting their boy-next-door quotient, lessening the threat posed by the leather and making the four of them seem more of a coherent whole. The Beatles were to be the first major band with a manufactured image. Epstein put them in suits. Not just any suits, but Beatle suits (based closely on a design by Pierre Cardin): a fairly tight-fitting jacket fastening to the neck with no collar, usually in black (though grey with black trim was also a characteristic Beatle look) with black or white turtle-neck sweaters or black tie on white shirt. The snappy look gained them not only publicity but imitators, among them the rest of Epstein's stable, including Gerry And The Pacemakers.

An early Beatles publicity still with the band in grey, two-piece suites inspired by Pierre Cardin

In the wake of the The Beatles a whole slew of Merseybeat bands emerged – many managed by Brian Epstein – and all dressed in sharp two-piece, three-button suits, often with velvet collars and pocket flaps. Witness: Billy J Kramer and The Dakotas

The other supergroup in embryo – and The Beatles' rough-edged competition – The Rolling Stones, followed suit in thin-lapelled two-piece styles. But they still all looked different. There was no attempt to sanitise them – quite the opposite. While Charlie Watts was ever the dapper gent, Bill Wyman might wear his with a leather waistcoat, Keith Richards in a state of general disarray. As Richards has said: "In those days you made a

Dougie Millings suits were cut to avoid cuff fray when playing guitar

"Brian Epstein had a tailor called Dougie Millings, who worked out of a shop above the Two IIs coffee shop in Soho, make up those collarless suits."

John and George in corduroy – the Beatles were credited with single-handedly saving the UK corduroy indusrtry

The Beatles in shiny two-tone, four button, velvet-collared suits based on the traditional English riding jacket. The more Mod two-tone suit gained wider popularity in the late 1970s with the ska movement, especially through graphic artist Jerry Dammers' styling of his band, The Specials. Dammers' 2-Tone record label and the strong black and white imagery of the movement boosted its appeal

"I think it's fair to say that they did steal that collarless look from Pierre Cardin. But their look did evolve from that. I was involved in making other funny collars for them at the time, and made the capes for *Help!*"

Top:
*The first man
of men's high
street fashion,
John Stephen*

Above:
*After Carnaby
Street had
seen its first
boutiques,
menswear
fashion shops
flowered
across Britain*

"It was really the shops of the times that led the bands and then the bands who made a particular look a mainstream fashion. The neat, Mod-inspired look was made by shops like Cecil Gee in Shaftsbury Avenue, boutiques in Carnaby Street, others like John Steven, Pauls, Lord John – they were all suppliers of the bands. Granny Takes A Trip on the King's Road was a big supplier of fashion to The Beatles and The Rolling Stones – Granny Takes A Trip sold real kaftans, for instance, beautiful, hand-made garments from Afghanistan with the tiny mirrors. You couldn't get them anywhere else. But then Lord John would get hold of the look and suddenly you had kaftans everywhere, albeit horrible ones, and the look went mainstream on the high street. Other influential shops of the time included Carrot On Wheels, Alsop Windle and Boyle and Hung On You – which got all of its wonderful fabrics from the old stock of this old department store-type of shop, called Pontins, I think, on Kensington High Street. Paul Reeves had a shop called the Universal Witness that I made a lot of clothes for in its early days – it sold clothes to Led Zeppelin and The Beatles, crushed velvet trousers and hand-appliqué shirts. Tommy Roberts had City Lights and before that Mr Freedom in Kensington Church Street, with a restaurant called Mr Feedem, which is a really bad name. They all made the looks that the bands took on, and that led to acceptance by the mainstream. These shop owners and designers were the unsung heroes of fashion."

Paul Smith

record and you'd see all these guys in brown coats walking around and pointing a microphone saying, 'Stand here and do this'. So we said, 'We'll just do what The Beatles don't.' It was like not wearing a uniform." As Mick Jagger added: "We used to think, 'We're not like these rock bands in sparkly jackets.'"

It was The Rolling Stones' approach that was to win out. Their dressing down of the suit – an approach which was to return in the Nineties – became a key look of the Sixties: The Animals, Them and The Kinks all took the decade's new tailoring – high-cut, wide-lapelled, double-breasted, narrow-legged – liberated to Carnaby Street from Savile Row, and made it their own with the American hippy aesthetic of wild flower-power shirts, floppy hats and Afghan coats. The approach was countered only by the Mods – a movement defined less by music and more by its sense of Italian dress. It was a style of narrow, fitted, almost minimalist jackets and short drainpipe trousers, often worn tieless with a shirt buttoned to the neck, adopted by The Who, The Small Faces (who even had their offices on Carnaby Street) and early Status Quo. Almost a counterpoint to the manipulation of

The Kinks in hunting gear - a departure from the Mod styling of the time though still showing a heightened appreciation of good tailoring. The Mod look was popularised by the likes of The Who and The Small Faces

The Stones never conformed to a group image. There's not a single suit in sight

Nik Cohn

"The Rolling Stones were the final destroyers of the gentleman, because they dressed at random. They set a stance of dissent."

"The Mod look was very functional in a way. The bum-freezer jacket with its double vents facilitated sitting on a scooter. It was derived from the British hunting jacket, of course."

Tom Gilbey

British Mods (inspired by Italian casualwear, short jackets with cutaway fronts and narrow lapels, slim trousers, tab-collar shirts and soft suede footwear) in Beatles-inspired jackets and boots

Epstein, The Who, when starting out, were co-managed by Pete Meaden, a leading 'face' of the original Mod movement who went on to shape the band and its look. Even the band's first single, as The High Numbers, was clothes inspired: 'I'm The Face/Zoot-Suit'.

Original soul stirrer Sam Cooke spent a lot of time and money on his clothes. The first black singer to cross-over from the gospel circuit to international pop stardom, Cooke started out wearing the uniform of nightclub respectability, the dinner suit, but swiftly took to crisp, dark, Mohair four-button two-pieces with creases sharp enough to cut yourself on. It was a look much imitated by nearly all the original Motown roster (Temptations, Four Tops, Miracles, Marvin Gaye) and other soul acts. His only near rival in the sartorial department was self-professed Soul Brother Number One James Brown, who favoured lighter coloured, often brown, velvet-collared three-piece suits which would have their flat-fronted trouser cuffs a good half inch above his ankle boots, and a darker waistcoat, sometimes in leather. Because the live performance circuit for soul acts throughout the Sixties remained the chicken-in-a-basket nightclub scene, soul performers tended to wear either evening suits or derivations of the same. Prior to the British Invasion of the US in the mid-Sixties, when The Beatles and The Stones booked black acts as support for their individual tours, soul and R&B acts were rarely seen on the same stage as white rock acts. Even then the likes of The Ronettes,

The sharpest dressed soul singer ever – Sam Cooke

Facing page:
James Brown demonstrating steps in a fine bum-freezer jacketed, three-piece in wool pinstripe

Left:
James Brown dressed like an English gent in bespoke three-piece suits, which were definitely not a la mode circa 1964

The Stylistics in dinner suit as a statement

Bo Diddley and The Crystals had to wear evening dress. It took stars of the stature of Cooke and Ray Charles or Little Stevie Wonder to break out of the dinner suit mould and be seen in sharp-cut Mohair two-piece suits on stage and then on album covers.

Even by the Seventies, however, the dinner suit, or rather derivations of it, were still being worn by soul acts on stage and television. The Chi-Lites, Miracles, Stylistics, Blue Notes, Drifters, Gladys Knight And The Pips and Delfonics among others were to be seen strutting their funky formation-dancing stuff wearing brightly coloured flared dinner suits with heavy piping, over ridiculously frilly-fronted shirts and stack heels. It was hard to tell, but there might have been a hint of irony in the overstated style.

But then, the early Seventies saw the kind of off-beat dressing-up-box playfulness with suits that characterised rock fashion in general. Abba and Status Quo took to denim suits; Gary Glitter wore sequinned numbers with launch-pads for shoulders; Mud and Showaddywaddy glammed it up with

The Chi-Lites in tailored three-piece suits exuding confidence

The suit didn't have to represent comformity or convention. Here, Teddy Pendergrass makes it casual, slick-suited and ready to lounge

Facing page: After Sam Cooke, Marvin Gaye was the best dressed singer in the world. This white tie and gingham waistcoat couldn't be worn by anybody else

Day-glo versions of the Teds' uniform; Bryan Ferry wore a GI uniform (in homage to the early Elvis perhaps?); Madness and The Specials bought tight, two-tone or mohair suits from second-hand stalls in Camden market; and so on. It was a mess of fashion outrageousness and contradiction. Rock stars either kept up with general trends or defined their own.

By the mid-Eighties, for many rock acts, the wearing of the suit proved their membership of the establishment, their final dance step away from the fickle young fashion crowd and towards an audience that didn't need its pop performers to be good looking, just well turned out, respectable, unthreatening and with a bit of rock 'n' roll history. Although rock suit wearers have come and gone – bands as diverse as The Kinks in flouncy Regency numbers and Depeche Mode in polyester, rolled-sleeve Don Johnsonesque Man-at-C&A styles have tinkered with a two-piece – by the middle of the Designer Decade a whole wave of once flamboyant wild men of rock had opted for a sober suit in which to do their increasingly routine business: Robert Palmer, Eric Clapton, Elton John, Phil Collins, David Bowie and Joe Cocker.

At the same time the serious suit had transplanted the dinner suit as the evening wear of choice for large, soul-singing men with large appetites: George Benson, Luther Vandross, Teddy Pendergrass and Alexander O'Neal all made their suits a classic smoothy soul garment. It was a look that Robert Palmer was to appropriate. Almost a parody of the impeccable, a caricature of a class-act, Palmer's wearing of the same get-up as Metallica – black tie and suit, white shirt (Palmer only ever wears white shirts) – in the video for his 1986 re-invention single

Robert Palmer in classic
English-inspired two-
piece with the Addicted
To Love backing band

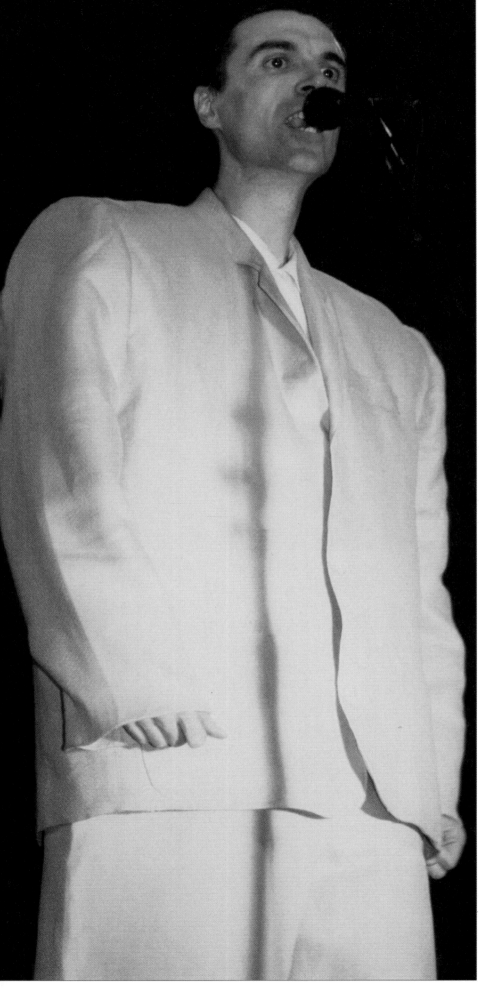

'Addicted To Love' was startling to the younger audience who had never heard of him. With the exception of his roguish looks and his being surrounded by a bevy of short-skirted and doe-eyed models, he could have been your dad. And yet, bewilderingly, somehow he looked cool. With three minutes of film, Palmer made the suit an acceptable fashion statement again. Over a decade later, the similarly, if more slickly, dressed Fun Lovin' Criminals owe their street-hustler chic not to Tarantino's *Reservoir Dogs*, but to Palmer.

It is all about wearing it right. The late Eighties and the Nineties saw the suit worn in a new way by some acts and in an old way by others. While some were able to pull it off with the panache of Sinatra and Dino – the Pet Shop Boys' Neil Tennant, for instance – others wore suits like a nasty case of the Claptons, because they were old or wanted the credibility of having made it through a rock life to become old. Phil Collins played Mr Ordinary and Eric Clapton donned glasses and suits as though sponsored by Armani – looking wide-shouldered and very corporate Eighties in a way parodied by Talking Heads' stylised nerd David Byrne and his outsize stage suit. Elton John's suits, of the colourful Versace persuasion, confirmed his place in the rockocracy as well as the real establishment as demonstrated by his friendship with (People's) Princess Diana, with whom he was so often snapped. And even George Michael – defiantly anti-image since going

Divine Comedy's Neil Hannon in Jasper Conran two-piece

George Michael out and relaxed in understated black suit

David Byrne in his 'Big Suit' box suit (it's not Armani)

The 1980s saw a revival of interest in the styles of post-War America – David Sylvian's outfit echoes the Zoot suit with its long drop at the front, while the slim lapels are more Teddy Boy style. The Bing Crosby-style bow-tie is typically 1940s, the make up pure 1980s

Suzi Quatro, the queen of the leather suit, all tight sleeves and flared legs

Kid Creole (with his Coconuts), the 1980s' premier zoot suit revivalist

The Jam in 1960s-inspired black suits, with unfeasibly wide flares

solo, singing on 'Freedom' how 'sometimes the clothes do not make the man' – adopted suits almost as a way of pursuing anonymity, if not to be taken seriously.

During the Nineties, the likes of pop acts Robbie Williams, Jay Kay of Jamiroquai and Pulp's Jarvis Cocker wore suits with some degree of tongue in chic. No matter how prepared they may have been to be taken home to mother, there was some sense of them playing with the codes of tailored suits. Furthermore, the late Nineties saw the suit worn casually for the first time since the Sixties. In an odd turn-up for the blokes, the suit which was once the mark of conformity – the word comes from the French *suivre*, to follow – was hijacked to become part of an alternative establishment, a pre-millennial rat pack. With work and home life increasingly blurred, the suit was casualised, an everyman outfit for the Beau Brummie, its re-appropriation by rock gods allowing them – as marketing strategies determined – to get closer to their audience.

The new wave of suits worn by rock stars in the late Nineties came about for much the same reasons as they were originally worn in the Fifties and early Sixties: so that the guys and gals who bought the records wouldn't feel closer to the high-flying, first-class-living and probably fabulously rich people who made them.

More Reservoir Dogs – aka Fun Lovin' Criminals

Facing page:
Suits needn't be smart citywear – rockers made them as wild as any other item in their wardrobe. Rod 'The Mod' Stewart's went for leopard print fur

Frank, Sammy, Dino and Peter Lawford, the Rat pack lounging. Who wouldn't want their style?

Puff Daddy does the gangsta thang

Following page: Sigue Sigue Sputnik mixing 1980s new rockabilly chic – borrowed from the 1950s American casualwear popularised at the time by Eddy Cochran – with space age punk

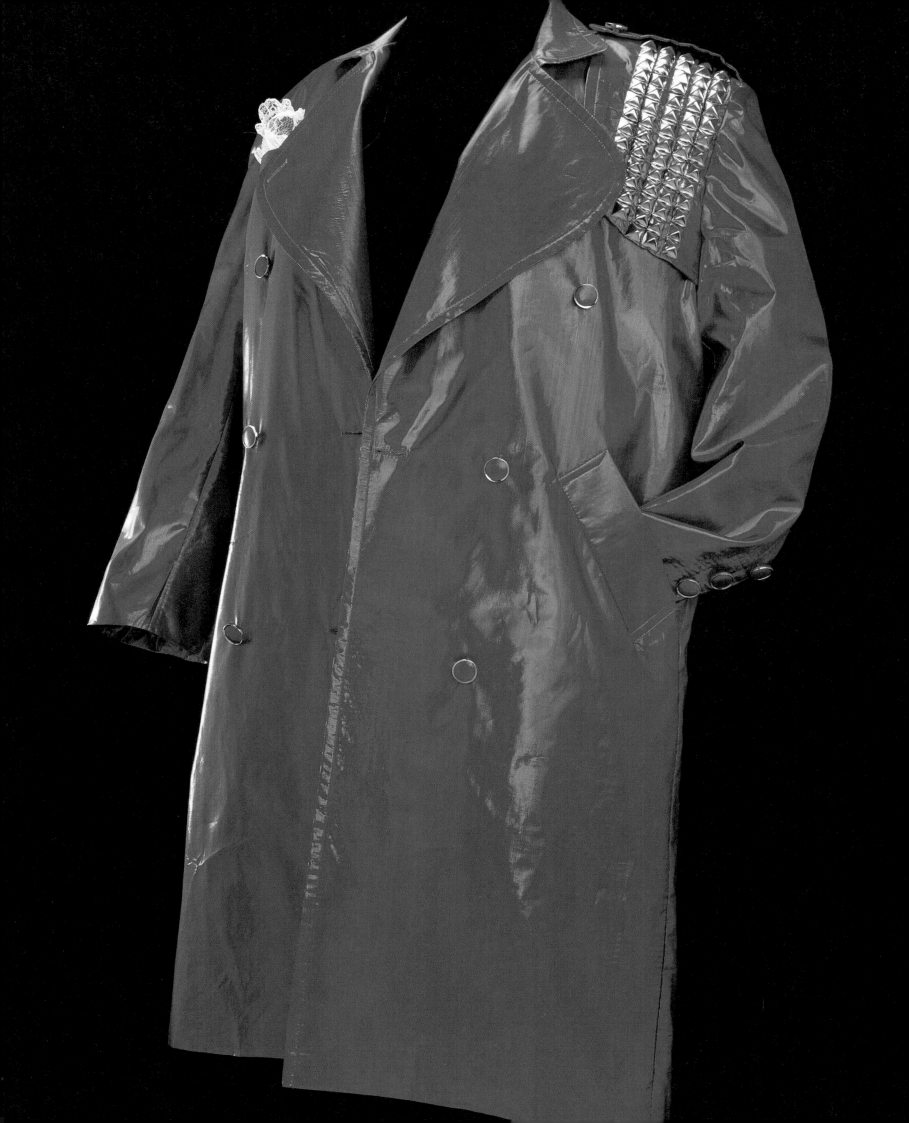

jackets

More so even than the suit, the tailored jacket has come to signify conformity, suburban inoffensiveness, the middle of the road. The jacket is worn over Argyle sweaters, with grey slacks. This jacket is not rock 'n' roll. And yet every act of the Fifties, from Hank Williams to Chuck Berry, Buddy Holly to Elvis, wore one. And they wore it well. In America it was known as the sports jacket, the one worn at weekends and in the evening in place of what was once the smoking jacket. Dino, Frank and Sammy wore them in films with open-neck shirts, sweaters and Mary Jane loafers, in the process imbuing the sports jacket with a sense of cool that would have a lasting effect on many rock 'n' rollers. In Britain, the jacket was an item of class identification. Working men would don an old tweed or herringbone on top of overalls to go to and from work; the middle-classes would only wear them at weekends; the upper-classes to ride and hunt (hence the sports tag).

Bill Haley's plaid was the showman side of Teddy Boy dress

Yet the rockers somehow made the jacket look different. In America, the country and western swing scene had created some fancy versions of the dinner jacket – the most famous 'customizer' of jackets and suits being the Nashville-based tailor Nudie, who made all of Hank Williams' outfits – and all of the touring showbands of the time wore velvet-collared, long-drop one- or two-button jackets over either matching or contrasting trousers. Bill Hayley, arriving in England in 1958 to resurrect his flagging career,

James Brown – in a sharp mohair jacket with shirt collar flying

"Tartan has a purpose in every walk of life. It really rocks on stage – from Bill Haley and his Comets to the Bay City Rollers and Rod Stewart all the way to The Sex Pistols."

Tommy Hilfiger

Facing page: The jacket did not have to be a sign of conformity. In the rock star wardrobe, it could be as loud as a heavy metal riff, as Prince's Sign Of The Times *tour jacket shows*

The jacket was no hindrance to Elvis Presley's performance

found that his checked jackets bore a close resemblance to the Edwardian frock coats favoured by Teddy boys – the Ted's adoption of an Edwardian upper class style being both aspirational and a chippy working-class statement of non-deference.

But, as with so much of rock history, it was Elvis who changed the way in which jackets were worn. In July 1956, mid-summer in Manhattan at the RCA Victor Studio One, Elvis recorded 'Anyway You Want Me' and 'Don't Be Cruel'. He had the star hair and white shoes and also had Argyle socks and a vented, single-breasted, two-button, brown, charcoal and black striped jacket. He looked good, both with the collar of his bright white shirt open and over the jacket's lapels, and with the lapels of the jacket turned up. It's a long way from the rhinestone white jumpsuit outfit he was to adopt twenty years later, but still somehow he doesn't look too respectable. It was a look that came to characterise the rest of Fifties menswear – the beginning of casualwear.

It was a look that didn't go away during the Sixties, an arch poise between sharp and sassy, simultaneously a look you could take home to your mother and a daddy-cool mockery of that notion. Pete Townshend of The Who made the jacket a one-off back-handed jibe at patriotism with his Union Jack number – a customisation of a standard item that has continued throughout rock history – Ian Dury, The Sex Pistols' Sid Vicious and John Lydon, and even AC/DC's schoolboy Angus being notable cases (not to mention the sequinned, studded, brocade or snake-skinned jackets of rock excess as worn by Jimi Hendrix and Lizard King Jim Morrison, Kiss and U2's Bono). But this waving of the flag was a reflection of the narrow-lapelled and high-notched Mod aesthetic as well, one also taken on by The Small Faces; one that shifted between the twin worlds of popular music and fashion.

Soul singer Joe Tex in 1967 – his attention to the details of dress was obsessive: the French cuffs, giant cuff-links, handkerchief and, above all, a high-notched, thin-lapelled jacket

The militaristic undertones of Jimmy Hendrix's brocade jacket, echoed in 1980s New Romantic style, were a pointedly ironic appropriation

Facing page: the jacket was taken up by working class Mods, among them bands such as The Small Faces, who helped overturn its usual class associations

The simplicity of jacket shapes in many ways proved a suitably blank canvas for many musicians to style in their own way – Stevie Wonder, jacket done up, tie loosened off

The Kinks – dedicated creators of fashion

Tom Gilbey, tailor

"I was asked to design a look for The Kinks and decided that a Regency look would go with their haircuts, so I made those high-collared jackets and put them with frilly-fronted shirts. I'm still owed £1,500 for doing that."

For the best part of the middle Sixties, the Mod jacket ruled: three-buttons, single-breasted, sloping shoulders, narrow-fitting, short and tapering to the hips, dark or striped and definitely not in sporty checks a la Elvis. It was a new school of dress popularised by the groups, affiliated to a strong youth movement, yet inoffensive to the older generation. American acts with easy access to TV danced and twisted away in similarly-cut styles.

The Kinks dressed in close-fitting double-breasted pea-coat style jackets, with dandy tone-on-tone shirt and tie sets

But that was to come: The Kinks typified the less austere Mod MkII/dandy element: it was their manager and agent Larry Page who signed the group to Pye Records in 1964 and put them in pink hunting jackets, a look abandoned the following year for the popular, though equally flamboyant, candy-stripe boating jacket style of the end of the decade that pre-figured hippy times (though the dress of the group's original bass player, Peter Quaife, stayed true to the Mod cause, and he even pottered between gigs on a Vespa GS scooter).

They looked decadent. By the standards of the day, they were. When asked to design a new look for them, Saville Row tailor Tom Gilbey took one look at their long page-boy hair and decided that Regency was the way to go. He gave them high collars with double-breasted fronts. The look was quickly picked up by high street stores across the country, even transferring to America where it was comparable to Navy-issue pea coats that filled Army and Navy surplus stores.

And because manager Brian Epstein had insisted that The Beatles wear matching suits, they also had to be seen in matching jackets. They were revolutionary in that both the collarless and Nehru collared jackets were a sight unseen on Main Street until the Fab Four wore them. Because they weren't the kind of thing you'd find in major menswear chain stores, men enlisted the relatively cheap services of specialist tailors to create the look. It proved the beginning of a revolution in menswear.

Prior to smartening up, of course, The Beatles had adopted Gene Vincent's 'dangerous' leather style. An early edition of *Mersey Beat*, the fanzine that followed the Liverpudlian groups in the early Sixties, best sums up the jacket's meaning: one photo captures Johnny And The Hurricanes in tailored jackets, with Johnny Guitar in a gold lamé shirt. They look tame. Next to them stand The Beatles, all in dark, aggressive leather. After five years of playing Liverpool and Hamburg they looked every inch the sensation they were to become… though, ironically, under manager Brian Epstein,

The Beatles - not quite dressed as a collective Fab Four, but definitely tailored to take home to mother

Gene Vincent in foreboding leathers. Even his limp added to his dark, menacing air

"It was dark when Gene's plane arrived at Heathrow. A delegation of us, including Joe Brown and the Bruvvers, met the plane on the tarmac. Airports were simpler in those days.

"As Gene loomed out of the darkness, his pale face, his polite, humble southern demeanour, his boring baseball jacket and his hobbling gait told me that I had a problem. Listening to Gene's records I had dreamed up the vision of a dangerous dagger-boy who could slit your throat as soon as look at you. Here instead was a young waif who looked as if he needed a nanny and a cup of cocoa.

"My background was the Shakespearean theatre, so I tried to imagine how Gene Vincent could be portrayed as an introverted villain. Black was the colour of introversion – Hamlet's inky cloak. The medallion around the neck came also with that role – as it did with that great Shakesperean villain, Richard the Third – who also had a limp. Leather, black leather, had been popularised by Marlon Brando in *The Wild Ones* – a film that had been banned in Britain and therefore was extremely noteworthy. The idea of the gloves came from a performance I had given at the Edinburgh Festival as the murderer Lightborn in *Edward II* by Marlowe. That production was designed by the brilliant Malcolm Pride who had given me gloves to wear for the murder of Edward. So I borrowed the idea for Gene."

Jack Good

they ditched the image in favour of The Hurricanes' tidy approach. Lennon reportedly hated the move while McCartney loved it, but away went the leather, the smoking and swearing and even eating on stage, and on came Beatle Boots, Pierre Cardin-inspired suits, mop tops and endless number ones.

Like rock itself, the leather jacket spoke to teenagers in a way that their parents didn't understand. Worn by the Teddy Boys' successors, the Rockers had, out of necessity – they all drove oil-spilling British bikes just like the one Marlon Brando rode in the then-banned film *The Wild Ones* – adopted Gene Vincent as their hero because he wore a Schott Perfecto. It was the spitting image of the one worn by Marlon. Ever since Brando had uttered the immortal reply 'Whaddya got?' to the question,

Rockers of the mid-1960s customised their jackets with badges, painted decorations and fabric patches showing their club affiliations. This more threatening look, readily picked up by rock stars, was a development of the simple, uncluttered army-surplus-based practical style of the so-called Ton-Up Boys (because of a penchant for riding their bikes at over 100 mph). Only their silky scarves showed an edge of fashion concern. Designers John Richmond, Katharine Hamnett and Pam Hogg have all created their own versions of the look

Luther Vandross, soul crooner, in designer leather, while Marvin Gaye's coat takes on more of a militant Black Panther look

'What are you rebelling against, Johnny?', troubled youth had associated the leather jacket with the thrill of danger and the sublime pain of being misunderstood.

Vincent wore black leather head to foot, including a ring over his one black glove, the jacket collar turned up and a DA in place. With his brace on show (Vincent had a limp as a result of a car accident), he looked positively creepy. This, after all, was a man black-listed by the US Musicians' Union for doing a runner with his band's pay and equipment. TV producer Jack Good knew exactly what he was doing when he insisted that the singer emphasise the limp as he moved around the stage during his first TV appearance on *Boy Meets Girls*. Watching teenagers would have wondered how he got the

The two Elvises: above, in tailored, smart, trimmed jacket and, left, making his comeback – and setting black leather in stone as the essential rock 'n' roll fabric

limp, what kind of a man he was to be able to sing about his baby in that eerie, reverb-laden voice.

After Vincent, the leather jacket became a rock 'n' roll cliché, and one that has never gone away. From Leonard Cohen to Suzi Quatro, Iggy Pop to Elvis Costello and Madonna to George Michael, the leather jacket has been the epitome of confrontational rock dressing, a levelling style as widely worn on the street by the fans as the star on the stage. Vincent was arguably the first to make leather part of the archetypal rock wardrobe, to make street wear an option for the stage – it was a look revived almost in every detail by Alvin Stardust fifteen years later when leather had gained more glamorous and less street-level associations. The result of Vincent's outfit was that he became a cult role-model for bad behaviour, notably in Britain, France and Germany (where black leather already had certain nationalistic connotations). Such was the power of Vincent's image that another act, Briton Vince Taylor, sued Vincent in a failed attempt to get him to stop wearing leathers.

Vincent's promotion of leather as the seminal rock 'n' roll material meant that even the King had, in 1968, to adopt the look for his NBC *Singer Special* comeback TV show. The producer of Presley's show decided that Elvis should go back to his rock roots because that was where he seemed most comfortable. Although Elvis never appeared in leather in the Fifties (except in one publicity still), it was decided that he must have invented the leather look, so a suit was duly made, albeit in contemporary

Robbie Williams dons leather jacket and trousers in homage to Elvis

style. (Thirty years later, in an act of absolute unoriginality, British pop star Robbie Williams appeared live on a British TV awards show wearing a leather suit that was the spitting image of Elvis'.)

With the close of the Sixties, all the old rules of dress had disappeared. Men no longer had to wear jackets in order to eat in restaurants, get into

clubs or watch sports. The world-wide adoption of leisurewear and unisex style had seen non-suit jackets and sports coats confined to the last few remaining gentlemen's outfitters still standing. By 1966, if a man wanted to wear a jacket, he could opt for a denim or corduroy blouson (see The Beatles in *Help!*), a Nehru-collared brocade velvet number, an antique bandsman's jacket (see Jimi Hendrix), a psychedelic peacock's take on a 1914 Royal Engineers jacket or countless leather styles.

By the beginning of the Seventies, the leather jacket had caught on in a big way, both with other rockers – Lou Reed's matched his eye make-up, Bob Dylan's blew in the wind, Jim Morrison's non-snakeskin version had collars as big as his Christ Complex, Bruce Springsteen's went with his New Jersey biker myth – and the public. But it wasn't to remain a mainstay of the rock wardrobe. While it has continued to tread the thin line between classic and cliché, the counter-cultural overtones of the black leather jacket were eventually countered. Punk returned it to street fashion at a time when rock stars were generally trying to distance themselves from their public again, to put on a show. The dressing-up of the glam era favoured jackets of an altogether less sober variety: Sweet and Gary Glitter's huge-shouldered Buck Rogers meets Busby Berkeley space-suit styles and Rick Wakeman's Ming the Merciless caped efforts were not exactly the kind of thing that would catch on with an adoring public. This was entertainment, not identification.

At first, punks wore the leather jacket as an ironic statement. Punk Perfecto's were daubed with slogans and studs in a slap-dash way which parodied the precise stud-work of Fifties Rockers and Sixties Hell's Angels. The Clash wore theirs in homage to Brando, Sid Vicious wore his

Early 20th century military jackets as worn by followers of late-1960s psychedelia and sold through shops such as I Was Lord Kitchener's Valet on London's Portobello and Carnaby Street

The Beatles take on the pick 'n' mix dress aesthetic of the late 1960s – any jacket goes

Convention meets revolution in Lou Reed's tailored leather jacket

The Boss in leathers for the cover of Born To Run

Andrew Loog Oldham, manager of The Rolling Stones

"Image can seize the first moment until substance is discovered, disciplined and developed."

Facing page:
The archetype of American rock, Bruce Springsteen, in biker jacket. The cover of his Born In The USA album encapsulated rock's love affir with that other American sartorial icon: denim

Following two pages:
The big bike-oriented greaser look, with customised and cut-down leather jacket, studs and German army helmet. And the essence of punk – spiky hair, but also the heavily personalised biker jacket

"Malcolm found some under-the-counter catalogues with examples of weird fetish-wear items and we started to crossbreed the biker look with this fetish wear. For example, we added multiple chains to jackets, or sadomasochistic flourishes and accessories to biker clothes."

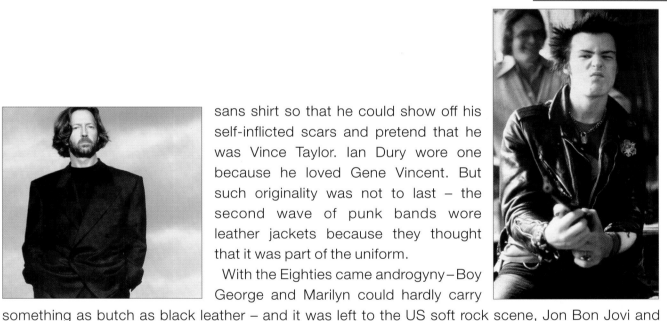

Sid Vicious – his jacket suited his bad attitude

Eric Clapton in Armani – the business suit for any aspiring MOR multi-millionaire rock star

sans shirt so that he could show off his self-inflicted scars and pretend that he was Vince Taylor. Ian Dury wore one because he loved Gene Vincent. But such originality was not to last – the second wave of punk bands wore leather jackets because they thought that it was part of the uniform.

With the Eighties came androgyny – Boy George and Marilyn could hardly carry something as butch as black leather – and it was left to the US soft rock scene, Jon Bon Jovi and Cher, together with the German leatherfest that was The Scorpions, to keep the leather flag flying.

The economic boom of the early Eighties and yuppie culture brought about a brief resurgence of interest in suits among rock stars, with some – Blue Rondo A La Turk and, most famously, Kid Creole's August Darnell – even resurrecting the zoot suit style. Once again, wearing single jackets with matching trousers became a norm both on stage and on the street. Horribly inspired by Don Johnson's appalling habit of rolling up the sleeves of his checked jackets in *Miami Vice*, both Dire Straits' Mark Knopfler and Phil Collins took to wearing their Armani jackets in a similar manner. Collins had been turned onto the understated but expensive appeal of Italian designers by Eric Clapton, who also rolled his sleeves up, although not too far. On the pop scene, the classic sports jacket was perverted by the likes of high-haired fashion disasters Howard Jones and Nik Kershaw, who sported three-button jackets in vile colours worn with cuffs rolled up, over t-shirts. For some reason, the

Rod Stewart when his Mod days had finally passed

Facing page:
The Beastie Boys

Previous two pages:
Jackets in their diverse rock guises – left page, clockwise from top: The Ramones, Suzi Quatro, Billy Idol and Don Letts. Right page, clockwise from top left: Gary Numan, New Romantics, Sid Vicious and Dire Straits

Michael Jackson in unusually restrained clothing – the brown leather jacket would soon be replaced by the more garish red and black style from Thriller

Matador madness from Bryan Ferry – fantastic stage wear

Eighties impressed upon everyone a need to make their clothes loud, colourful and over-stated. It almost killed off the jacket as an item for any discerning man's wardrobe.

George Michael attempted to do the same with the Perfecto. He managed to fool all of the people for a few years into thinking that his stubble, driving gloves, shades and leather jacket, as worn on the cover of *Faith*, made him a mean, moody, hetero hero. In the process he put all right-thinking persons off the idea of wearing a black leather jacket. Michael was assisted in the process of wrecking the reputation of the leather jacket by Michael Jackson. His eccentric dress sense veered undecidedly: *Thriller* saw the red and black, pointy-shouldered leather jacket that, indicative of how the Eighties matched the Seventies stitch for stitch in nasty clothes, actually saw imitations worn on the high street. *The Wedding Singer,* a late Nineties film that launched an Eighties retro appreciation, has one character turning up to a party in his MJ single glove and jacket: except that he's white, with a Village People moustache and a paunch. He doesn't quite carry it like Jacko. *Bad* had Jackson return to the standard biker fair, although he had more pockets than he has gold discs, a fact he parodies in 'Badder', the kids' spin-off video of the song.

Post-punk, leather faded. New Romanticism turned to costumiers to provide the ultimate stage paraphernalia: Sigue Sigue Sputnik, a kind of parody of Seventies dress-excess, wore their jackets cropped, sat below hairpieces built like exploding fireworks and perched above platforms high enough to make Gary Glitter lose his sparkle. Adam Ant, styled by Vivienne Westwood, hoisted the jolly roger in brocaded 19th century military jackets, cross-referenced less with Hendrix than Red

Art school grad and concept popster Adam Ant, self-styled with some direction from Malcolm McLaren and Vivienne Westwood, relished the decadence of late 1970s/early 1980s New Romanticism, inspired as much of the dress was by the heroic fantasy costume of 18th century highwaymen, pirates, rogues and dandies. Propelled by a burgeoning club scene, the movement's dress mixed references to both the past and the future and came as a counter to the street-level aggression and DIY dress of punk. For Adam Ant it culminated in the Westwood-designed outfit for the cover of the album Prince Charming *in 1982*

Facing page: arch smoothy Bryan Ferry in Anthony Price. The tieless shirt with done-up top-button was quintessential 1980s

"With Acid there was an emergence of young people who dressed to die for. Dressing was their art form, but you could number them on the fingers of one hand, at first. That burgeoned very quickly, people would see them on the street or in the Chelsea antique market and copy what they were wearing."

Christopher Gibbs, tailor

Indian tribal feathers and paint – about as romantic in its connotations of *Boys' Own* adventures and wild escapades as you could get. In short, visually stunning but not the way anybody was going to dress down the pub without leaving it badly bruised.

But fashion, even with pop stars, moves in cycles. And after twenty-odd years of avant-garde activist styling, the late Eighties and Nineties saw a shift back to the essential basics of Mod tailored jackets and black leather simplicity. But this was a defiantly casual, man-of-the-street jacket: the narrow-fitting Oxfam cast-offs of Jarvis Cocker, or Casual with a big C, Mancunian, with all the emphasis on labels – be they Stone Island or Lacoste. Terrace chic made the impossible happen: it

Marc Bolan of T Rex
in a leather jacket
looking forward to
Michael Jackson's
costume for his
Thriller video

made the windcheater part of the rock 'n' roll wardrobe. Fans didn't have to *try* to look like Oasis. Oasis made every effort (and not in a Machiavellian marketing way) to dress like their fans – because, like the punters, they were just Ordinary Joes, despite having a few million in the bank.

The jacket is the garment that exemplifies that vacillating need for rockers to be close to, and then distanced from, their record-buying public.

"Oasis connect with their fan base – young, working-class men – because those fans can picture themselves in Liam Gallagher's shoes, both literally and metaphorically. Oasis *are* their fan base – they're young, working class men. The band and its look has grown out of the environment it appeals to, rather than having to invent one."

Simon Jordan of youth communications agency Magic Hat

The boys next door style of Oasis – their dress has been carefully considered, even if it doesn't look it

"We sell lots of clothes to rock stars: Bowie, Jagger and younger groups like Oasis, Texas. But now the bands are just buying clothes. They're stylish people but they're not wearing rock star clothes, silver jackets or frock coats, just clothes that are available to the public."

Paul Smith

Abba – the undisputed kings and queens of 1970s fashion

Carnaby Street: Centre of the universe for 1960s fashion

"I lost interest in rock stars as a species in about 1966, when it became clear that rock 'n' roll had been absorbed into the establishment, into mainstream commercialism and had been quietly castrated in the process.

"We had Carnaby Street, Mersey Beat (whose father was not, as it is claimed, Chuck Berry, but rather George Formby – can't you just hear our George singing 'When I'm Sixty-Four'?) and the British Invasion in which a bunch of cutely-dressed, fresh-faced pseudo-rockers with those cute English accents bowled over millions of mindless American teeny-boppers in their training bras and pseudo-Mary Quantery. Suddenly the curtain fell on the real rock 'n' roll scene with its real rock 'n' roll stars – Jerry Lee, Little Richard, Carl Perkins, Fats Domino, Chuck Berry. They were overshadowed by the tailor's dummies from Penny Lane.

"Rock (as it was now called) had become trendy – and the cute, Cuban-heeled, bob-cut, bob-kittens from *Ready, Steady Go*ville became the supreme arbiters of taste. The rock fans stopped being the rebellious underdogs and became dedicated followers of fashion: mild, milksop mods on their motor-scooters zooming down to Southend in order to make a splash in the *Daily Mirror*."

Jack Good, pop impresario and manager of Gene Vincent

A young Duran Duran delighting in New Romanticism's dressing up

Elton John with designers Donatella and Santo Versace

67 jackets

Following pages: *Psychedelic peacocks.*
Left: *Mitch Mitchell's hand painted jacket, 1967*
Right: *Jimi Hendrix's peacock feather waistcoat, 1968.*

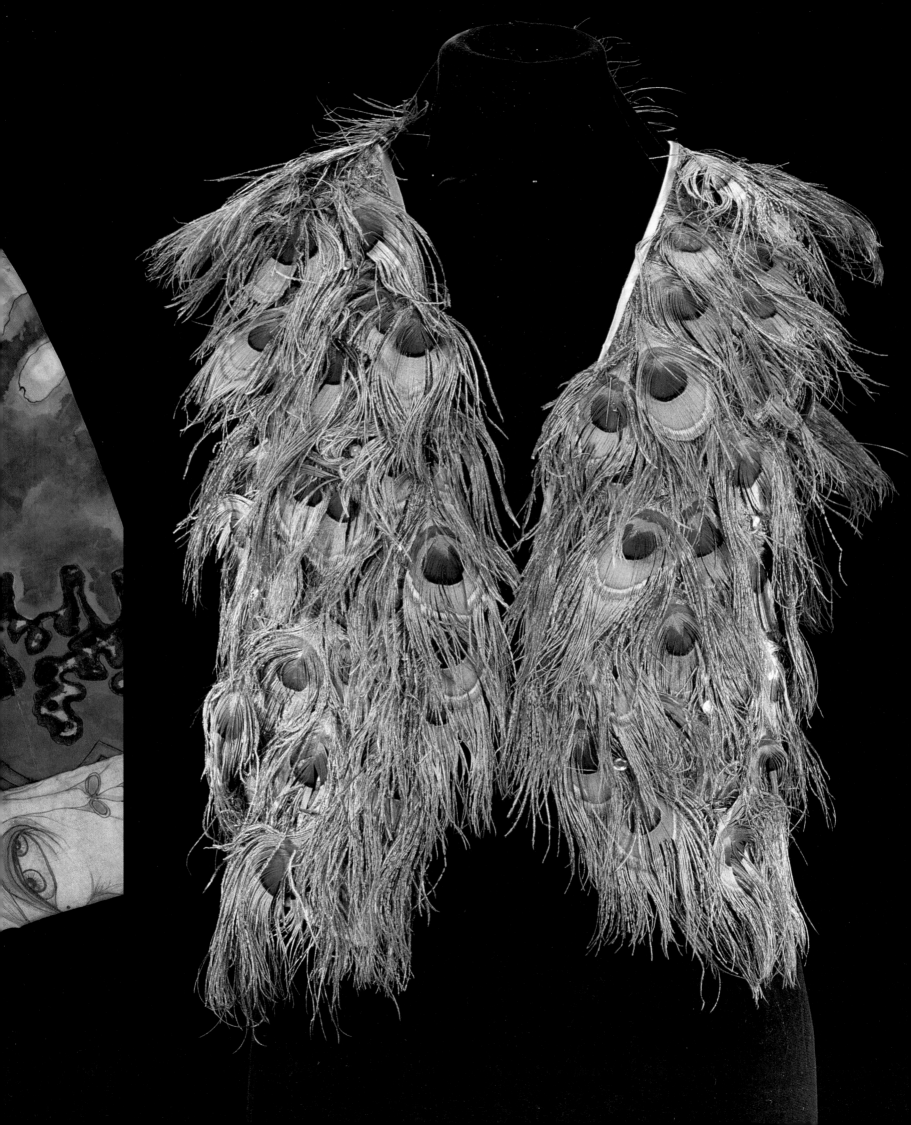

The moment that black became the colour of cool

"Elvis in 1956 is a defining image for the twentieth century, along with Marilyn Monroe with her skirt blowing up or Marlon Brando in the leather jacket from *The Wild Ones*."

Tom Gilby

trousers|shirts

The King relaxes in a Cadillac, wearing blouson style jacket, mohair trousers and silk shirt

In the Fifties, it was rare to see a man on stage without a jacket, dressed in only trousers and a shirt. Dino, Frank and even Hank (Williams) always either kept on their DJs or wore sweaters, cardigans, waistcoats. Anything to retain that aura of cool ineffability. As with everything else, Elvis changed that. Because he moved so much while performing, and because his hips moved so much in particular, he would at some point during a performance take off his jacket and continue singing, gyrating and strumming.

There's little doubt that the Elvis moves were all of his own, just as there's no doubt that his choice of stage and leisure wear was (until 1958, at least) all his own. His choice of trouser style was perfect for showing off his wild pelvic wriggle while hinting at what was behind the pleated front tapering to 12-inch cuffs. His trousers in 1956 were slightly less exaggerated versions of the zoot suit style, designed to accentuate his slim hips. When worn with a padded-shouldered sports jacket, they gave the triangle shape so beloved of hipsters at the time.

The coolest knitwear model ever

Elvis' shirts echoed the slightly fey, flamboyant style of pimps and hustlers of the day. Whether in black, white or pink, they were usually wide-collared, unbuttoned – whether worn with a tie or without – and made of a cotton soft enough to hang loose without crumpling. Later of course, the shirts would be made of silk.

One of the earliest defining images of rock music is that of Elvis twisted around a microphone stand, his right leg turning on the toe point, his right arm raised, back slightly arched and quiff falling. The shape made by the black trousers and shirt is

Facing page: Roger Daltrey's stage jumpsuit from the early 1970s in chamois leather. Presumably for The Who's cover of 'When I'm Cleaning Windows'

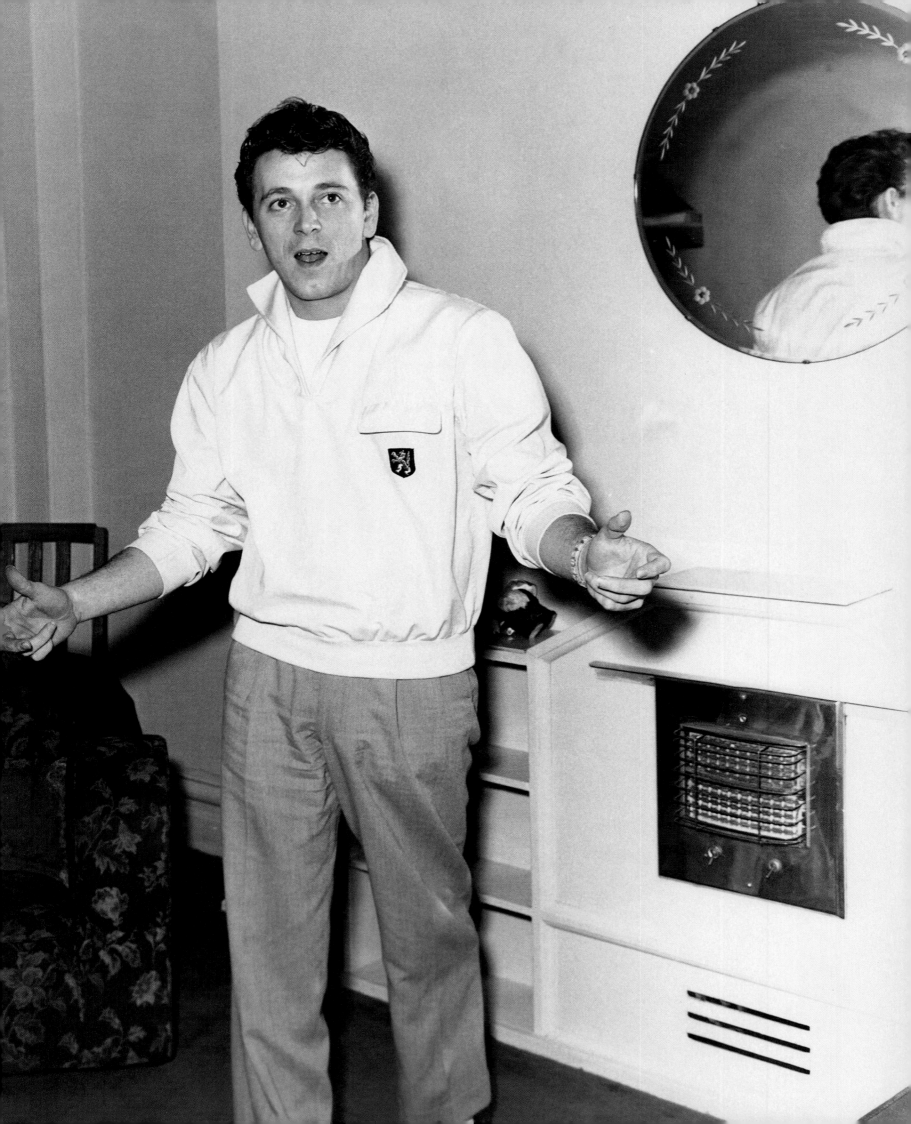

fluid and yet sharp. Future generations of rock performers would attempt to emulate that move and look for the next four decades.

Among the wave of Elvis imitators that followed, a few notable performers would have a profound effect on fashion. Cliff Richard's black shirt and white tie proved irresistible to British Teddy Boys and wannabe spivs at the time, while Gene Vincent's first incarnation as a Blue Cap began a trend for bowling shirts that would be revived at regular intervals well after the game had lost its appeal. Through the inspiration of British TV producer Jack Good, Gene Vincent would later create a particular rock fashion cliché that shows no sign of losing its allure forty years after it first appeared.

In 1959 Vincent's career in his homeland America was on the wane. He'd split with his band and record sales were dipping. So, just as Bill Haley had done the year before, he travelled to England to a rapturous welcome from the Teds and their new offshoot brethren, the Rockers, who regarded him, and rock's other working-class hero, Eddie Cochran, as the real deal. Vincent met Good when the latter was producing UK TV music show *Boys Meets Girls*. Jack Good had previously imbued mild-mannered Billy Fury with an edge of danger that made the girls scream and the boys respect him enough to buy his records in droves (he had also put Fury in a gold lamé jacket for one appearance on TV and filmed him from below his crotch in another). Good understood that girls liked the wrong

Silk polka-dot shirt, sharkskin trousers and, er, headscarf for dancing in the aisles mid-Fifties America style

Facing page: Pre-leather, Gene Vincent in narrow-leg pegs and sweater top

*Jerry Lee Lewis –
in the mid-1950s
only Elvis could
rock harder and
dress better*

Jack Good

"I was deeply interested and involved in the costumes for *Catch My Soul* which was, in case you hadn't noticed, rocky but very hirsute – as opposed to *Jesus Christ Superstar* which was not only unrocky, hirsute and heretical but very, very, boring to boot.

"For the Los Angeles premiere of *Catch My Soul* at the Ahmanson Theatre, I employed the noted designer, Ray Agahyan, to create the costumes. I wanted the colours and textures of the painter Rouault and the style of the wild hippies at the Renaissance Fair in Chatsworth. I got what I wanted in spades – and hearts, too. To see Jerry Lee Lewis as Iago in Ray Agahyan's costume is to have lived."

"The Doors of Perception were flung open and everybody in the rock scene was liberated. They would no longer conform. Everyone henceforward would be totally free and would do his own thing. The rock world became a fancy-dress ball to which all were invited to come as they pleased. The curious thing was that this liberated bunch of freaks all came to the ball wearing nearly identical costumes, topped by nearly identical masses of flowing hair.

"Hippiedom was the most rigorously comformist society the world had seen and the 'Peace-and-Love' Fashion Fascists had no time for anyone over thirty in a grey suit: i.e. me. Frankly, my dear, I didn't give a damn.

"I still got work and was able to vent my spleen by satirising the Swingin' Sixties in a series of Hollywood TV specials in which the people I was poking fun at willlingly appeared, blinded by smoke and self-importance to the fact that they were my targets. Oh joy, oh bliss, oh poop-poop!"

Jack Good

sort of boys. He dressed Vincent (who already had something of a reputation as a wild man after rumours about a US tour involving hotel wrecking leaked out) in all black leather in an echo of Rocker style, and told the former US Navy motorcycle dispatch rider to emphasise a limp he'd developed as a result of a bike accident four years earlier. The result was instant acclaim and success for the singer, and an eternal connection between leather trousers and dangerous rock stars.

It was Jim Morrison, singer with The Doors, who really made leather trousers an absolute cliché. Blessed with extreme good looks, convinced he had the romantic soul of an eighteenth-century poet and fronting a band who dared to fly in the face of contemporary musical fashion, he became an instant star when first seen on TV on the *Ed Sullivan Show* in 1967. His tight leather trousers and tumbling curls, combined with the fact that, when asked to change the line 'Girl we couldn't get much higher' in 'Light My Fire' Morrison insisted on keeping it in, made him both an idol to millions of watching teenage girls, and also their elder brothers. It was a dichotomy which would anger Morrison until his early death aged 27 in 1971. Doors audiences were a strange mixture of screaming schoolgirls and the emerging generation of Americans who were latching onto the spirit of revolution and protest that was disrupting college campuses across the nation. Not that it stopped him taking advantage of his rock sex god status. It wasn't until 1970, when Morrison had grown an untidy beard and was quite fat, that he stopped wearing the leather trousers, snakeskin boots and open-to-the-navel white shirts in which he was immortalised on innumerable bedroom walls. By then it was too late. Countless scores of rock singers and even guitarists had bought a pair in the hope that instant sex god status would be bestowed upon them; for the most part it didn't work. Rick James, Slash of Guns 'N Roses, the Clash's Mick Jones and Frankie Goes To Hollywood's Paul Rutherford were just some who dared take the stage in hide strides. Elvis, of course, famously donned a pair for his 1968 NBC TV 'Singer

Tommy Hilfiger with Goldie

Tommy Hilfiger: Would you wear this man's name on your back – or your underwear?

"**Fashion is for followers, for conformists, for people who are unsure of their own identity, for, in a word, 'twits'. I despise fashion. Especially today when the twits are walking adverts for the even more twittish designers. There was a day when the cut and cloth of your suit spoke for its origin. Nowadays the twits and twittesses boogie around with sloppy clothes that yell 'Tommy Hilfiger' at you! Tommy who? Tommy why? And I am expected to pay more for a garment advertising this Tommy fellow than an identical garment without his name splashed over it? The world has gone stark, staring mad.**"

Jack Good

Special' comeback appearance but his were worn with a leather jacket and both finely cut in a contemporary style which owed nothing to Morrison's Byronic Lizard King persona.

The only other trouser legacy of Elvis' in the Sixties proved to be chinos and Farrah slacks, which he wore in several of his films. Both the flat-fronted chinos and Farrah slacks would, by the middle of the decade, become a part of the 'classic' All-American WASP look for weekend wear (always combined with Brooks Brothers button-down collar shirts, tan Bass Weejun loafers and sweater). Mods in the UK went for the clean, sharply-creased Farrahs while hippies went for the crumpled US Army-style chinos. More than twenty years later both Tommy Hilfiger and Ralph Lauren would make the style a multi-million dollar staple of their clothing empires.

While Morrison was building a popular association between leather, sex and wild, debauched behaviour in California, across the country in New York another bunch of rock 'n' roll degenerates were creeping around on stage wearing tight black or white Levis, black polo-neck sweaters and wraparound sunglasses. Oddly, perhaps, given their name, The Velvet Underground never went in for either leather or rubber fetish wear on stage, and, perhaps more strangely, Andy Warhol doesn't seem to have suggested it, either. Which is possibly why they never enjoyed the kind of teen fan base

While the world put on psychedelic coloured flares, the Underground (and Andy Warhol) went for black and white straight-legged jeans. Nico (far left) added a chic white trouser suit

The Who in carefully ironed 'mod' clothes: arrow and bulls-eye jumpers and drainpipe Sta Prest

"When I was 17, 18, I listened exclusively to black music but looked to the white British bands for fashion. It wasn't that you slavishly copied – though I have to confess once painting targets and symbols onto an old cotton jacket after the style of The Who – it was more like checking yourself in a mirror, to be sure you'd got nothing wrong. These were bands like The Who, Small Faces, Stones, even The Beatles (but not the silly jackets). There were no style sections in newspapers to help you, just the obscure corners of the weekly music press at a time when the music editors were clueless as to what was really going on. Then there was a period when fashion, specifically Mod fashion, which was the only one that counted, moved ahead of the groups instead of following."

Nick Logan

The Doors accumulated. Clearly, Warhol had suggested the polo-neck sweater look – later re-created by Michael Fish for the casino and disco crowds of London and New York in the winter of 1967 which proved a major success. Warhol himself took to them with gusto and was thereafter rarely photographed wearing anything else.

In the Fifties and Sixties, leather and denim were firmly considered workwear material only. British rockers and American Hells Angels took the materials on to new levels of association, none of which were considered glamorous. Just as Gene Vincent was the first performer to take leather on to the stage, Eddie Cochran was the first rock 'n' roller to wear denim jeans as a fashion item. Although Woody Guthrie and assorted other folk protest singers of the Thirties and Forties had worn denim suits and overalls, they did so out of a sense of solidarity with the poor working man whose oppression inspired their songs. Cochran wore his so that he could suggest James Dean as he stood, one thumb hooked in the hip pocket, and belted out 'Twenty Flight Rock'. Cochran was the first rocker to use the bored teenager persona as a marketing tool. His white T-shirt and jeans ensemble reflected what he said in song: ain't no cure for the summertime blues, so I don't give a fuck. Eighteen years after Cochran's death in an automobile accident which also saw Gene Vincent injured, the punk scene's very own mixed-up bored teenager Sid Vicious would dress up in a white tuxedo and black zip-covered jeans to belt out two Cochran hits, 'C'Mon Everybody ' and 'Somethin' Else'.

The Mod movement made the wearing of non-suit or dresswear trousers a standard when they adopted Sta Prest and flat-fronted Levis into their dress code. This prompted The Who to wear clean jeans on stage, although it would be another few years before singer Roger Daltrey would swap his

white Sta Prest for faded denim flares. Daltrey, to his credit, first wore flares in the mid-Sixties, long before they became a common sight, at a time when only a small coterie of West London faces knew where to buy them.

As their name suggest, The Small Faces were Mod-obsessives. Singer Steve Marriott and bassist Ronnie Lane in particular were determined to have the best, newest and sharpest clobber they could get their hands on. Almost permanent habitués of the first non-chain menswear stores to stock continental designs, they would wander around Lord John's for hours, picking up items and demanding them all. Lane was particularly taken with a range of polka-dot shirts which featured a different colour collar. The design was soon adopted across the UK.

Denim only really became a cloth to be worn on stage when the idea of stage clothes became unhip and the 'serious' side of the music business decided that fashion was too shallow to be bothered

"I had a phone call from Lord John saying that Ronnie Lane wanted to buy some shirts. I said, 'Fine, let him have them, we'll pay.' And they replied, 'Well, he wants all of them. There's a hundred.' We had them delivered to the office, they were piled up in a corner. Ronnie couldn't have someone else wearing the same shirt as him."

Tony Calder

The Small Faces on one of their shopping trips to Lord John, Carnaby Street

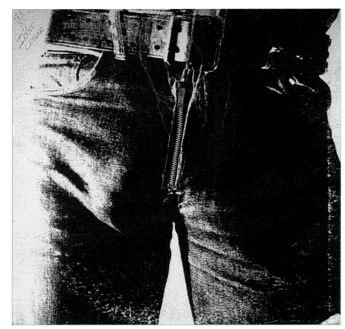

"I like to see jeans worn with a thick, heavy-duty leather belt or webbed fabric, as worn in the military. The buckle should be solid, like double d-rings or old western buckles. Remember the double-prong belt buckle on the cover of The Rolling Stones' Sticky Fingers? That was the coolest."

Tommy Hilfiger

with. A generation of love-and-peace-influenced young Americans had worn jeans for the past five years, rarely, if ever, dressing in either formal or work wear. Jeans were the gear one wore to tune in, turn on and drop out, because they were hard wearing, relatively cheap and unisex. Andy Warhol, always a man to exploit an undiscovered area of possibility, attempted, with his work for a then decidedly drug-influenced Rolling Stones, to make an ironic art statement out of his design for the cover of their *Sticky Fingers* album cover. It depicted a jean crotch shot complete with working zip that, when pulled down, showed a small patch of pubic hairs. The cover said cool, sex, rebellion, one of us. The music said stoned, out of it on Class A stuff. All of which was very cool, of course.

By the early Seventies, heavy rock and progressive rock's uniform consisted of dirty flared jeans, washed-out T-shirts and long, unkempt hair. Bands such as Pink Floyd and Yes were uninterested in being stars in the Morrison mould, they just wanted to make music, man. Oh, and have thousands of lights and special effects, of course, to detract from the fact that they looked like they'd slept in the same clothes for a week.

American acts such as The Eagles opted for all-denim uniforms which were of similar style to those worn by various funk outfits, but looked somehow far more drab, despite the cowboy overtones.

Glam brought some much-needed colour to the music scene in the early Seventies. Shirts had to be bright and have large collars and preferably flared sleeves, trousers had to have minimum 24-inch flares and patch pockets. Unless you were Brian Eno or Bryan Ferry, in which case you wore imitation Flash Gordon outfits. Or David Bowie, who wore strange

tights and leotard outfits until he discovered soul music for *Young Americans* in 1975, when he donned a pair of the baggiest trousers ever seen. Cut with an astonishing twenty-four pleats and tapering to ankle-width, they were an exaggeration of the Oxford Bag style so beloved of white soul boys at the time (Forties-style heavy trousers that hung parallel to the pleat and were not flared). Bowie topped the trousers with a voluminous white shirt with military-style pockets and a wedge haircut. Again a reflection of what was happening at soul clubs in England's South East.

By the time punk happened, people either wore jeans or Bags or loon pants or… anything as long as it was flared.

*David Bowie in
Soul Boy guise,
complete with
flared hips*

*Ginger Baker, Eric
Clapton and Jack
Bruce (Cream) on
a bad hair day*

Which is why punk trousers had to be straight: punk was anti everything. Jim Morrison's trousers were one of the first rock clichés that punk parodied. Instead of leather, Rotten's trousers were plastic. For no reason other than it looked weird and parodied the idea of functional work clothes, zips were sewn onto trousers and jeans. Because Sex was selling fetish wear, Westwood added bondage straps to tartan straight-leg trousers.

The 'official' punk look as decreed by McLaren and Westwood was PVC shiny (it washed down easily), zippered and adorned with offensive images. Johnny Rotten was arrested for wearing a Sex T-shirt which depicted two cowboys facing each other their penises almost touching. Siouxsie Sioux goose-stepped about in peg-fronted trousers wearing a swastika armband. The clothes of the establishment, including elements of school uniforms, were worn in a way that mocked what they represented. It was all tight, dark and aggressive, an anarchic contrast to the Sixties billowing and floral dress of the flower power protest singers; punk, in contrast, stood for nothing. Anything trashy or widely considered tasteless – plastic, PVC, leopard-skin prints – was adopted by the punk movement. Hair and make-up was coloured and extreme, not to enhance but to startle, the sexual

Former Sex shopgirl Jordan modelling vintage Westwood bondage trousers

Vivienne Westwood's infamous Cowboys T-shirt

Lots of punks were still at school in 1976, thus the uniform they wore every day was the only item of clothing they could customise into punk gear (the prices in Sex, Seditionaries and Boy were prohibitive to anyone dressing on £5 a week pocket money)

That nice Mr Rotten modelling Uncle Talcy Malcy's latest bondage gear for the Sex catalogue, 1977

"We started to put zips in odd places where they shouldn't logically be. We thought about the construction of clothes. What was a zip for, anyway? After all, there were all sorts of other sexy associations to do with zips."

Vivienne Westwood

In 1966 Jim Morrison posed naked from the waist up, leather trousers from the waist down as if crucified. Ten years later Johnny Rotten made a typically ironic punk statement. Can you tell what it is, boys and girls?

Unlike the Pistols,
The Clash
couldn't cadge
clothes from
their manager's
Chelsea boutique.
They made
their own

"The relationship between music and fashion is more of a two-way street now. It works in both directions. That hasn't always been the case. It's a fact that on all the magazines I've edited – from *NME* onwards – musicians' attitudes, and their clothes in a secondary way, have been an important factor. On the *NME* I practically banned live-in-concert photography, or at least relegated it to the reviews section. Live shots, despite claims made for them, are for the most part banal. The really iconic stuff – Pennie Smith's seminal shots of The Clash or Roxy Music for the *NME* for instance – usually gets produced away from the stage. The Sex Pistols were maybe an exception, they never took a bad shot anywhere."

Nick Logan

The Clash, a perfect punk fashion statement: Home-sewn zips, hand-stencilled shirts and self-mutilated hair.

Cher in an original Sex Pistols T-shirt from Sex

connotations of skirts or trousers draped in chains, was an aesthetic of deviancy. It was deliberately ugly, an image so strong that in later years it was ripe for parody, the ideal notion of street-style but also the ideal fancy dress outfit.

The Clash made their own clothes. Taking a lead from his beloved reggae albums, bassist Paul Simonon stencilled slogans and song titles to the band's black and white shirts, turning them from the mundane to spectacular propaganda tools. Simonon and Strummer took genuine workman's overalls and hammered the zips and cloth in a local

Following pages:
Two pictures from
roughly the same
time. Left; disco
dancers. Right;
Sid and Nancy

Mod revival Mk I. The Jam in bum-freezer suits, flares, baseball boots and Doc Marten's.

car workshop to give them a lived-in look before spraying slogans across them. The Clash were the inspiration to subvert their own clothing for thousands of punks without the cash to spend at Sex or other Chelsea punk shops. Strummer was also the first to start a trend for army combat trousers by wearing them on stage and in an infamous photo-shoot on Belfast's Falls Road in 1977.

Punk was a seminal moment for trousers in the history of rock fashion, banishing the flare from sight in the UK (although it took a few more years in America, where the 1978 film *Saturday Night Fever* showed flares galore among the disco dancers). However, the musical and fashion movement which followed it was the era of the shirt. New Romanticism flounced onto the scene in November 1979, almost two years after The Sex Pistols had called it a day. At the time the Mod scene was making a comeback thanks to The Jam, while The Police were regularly raiding the charts and an underground scene was giving rise to the likes of Joy Division and Simple Minds. None of them looked anything special. Sting sang in some interesting sweaters (a stripy, bumble-bee look gave him

New Romantics
mixed historically
inaccurate
flourishes with
streetwear

his nick-name, or so the story has it) and The Jam
followed the Mod aesthetic – trousers tight and
bum freezer jackets. But most of these bands
made a point of looking ordinary: Joy Division
notably to the point of anonymity.

But not the New Romantics. This was music as
escapism, with a look to match. While punk
pursued a dress policy of nihilism, the New
Romantics paid close attention to every detail.
Originally the movement was called the Blitz
Kids, after the London club which gave birth to
the scene which mixed avant-garde hairstyles

The Beatles post-marijuana period

Brian Jones

U.S. advertising using neo-Dandy pop styling to sell shoes

with a Victorian theatricality of dress. Their shirts were artworks. If for the rock stars before them – the Stones, The Beatles – the shirt was largely a question of tidy conformity or, with The Monkees, orchestrated mother's boy cuteness, soon to be abandoned once established for wilder, less establishment designs, for New Romantics the shirt went against the norm from the start. Groups such as Duran Duran, Visage and Classix Nouveau wore Lord Byron styles like they were going out of fashion. Which they were. Shirts like big girls' blouses had been made to look normal on rock 'n' rollers since the late Sixties, but the New Romantics were to prove new kings of the frill.

The look perfectly suited the Duran Duran approach: despite hailing from Birmingham, theirs was a new kind of rock 'n' roll excess, one more concerned with yachts, fast cars and faster supermodel girlfriends than throwing TVs into the pool. Perfect for the advent of the MTV video age – when rock fashion became more an issue of a band's corporate image rather than an element of their unique self-expression – Duran Duran's videos for 'Girls On Film' and 'Wild Boys' were Spielbergian in their gloss of expensive other-worldliness. Nick Rhodes' non-smudge mascara and pan-cake foundation, the band's mix of tight black leather trousers, giant white shirts (tucked in), and giant hair (with more

"Brian is up there, and Mick, although Mick was a delicate and beautiful creature. Brian was sturdier and into straight fancy dress and flouting all perceived wisdom about what to wear. He was into ethnic clothes much earlier than most other rock people."

Christopher Gibbs

mousse than Alaska) equally so. They were not of Planet Earth.

But one band was to typify the movement's fashion – and inspire fan imitation – more than any other: Spandau Ballet. A spin-off of a group called The Makers, Spandau were apparently inspired by a trip to Berlin, though their dress became about as far from any Bauhaus aesthetic as you could get. At its height, Spandau Ballet's lead singer Tony Hadley was earning over £120,000 a year. By the late Nineties he was broke. It looked as if most of his cash went on shirts. Despite having emerged from a terminally fashion-conscious dance club scene, Spandau Ballet, Gary Kemp was to explain, 'Never intended to create an artificial front for the band. We are what we are.' That being

*Duran Duran. It's
okay. They're
from Birmingham*

Spandau Ballet's Tony Hadley looking for the audition for an ITV adaptation of Shakespeare

a bunch of men so dress-consciousness that they had their own stylists before being signed to any label. They even went as far as to reject Island Records' approach for a contract on the grounds that they didn't want to risk losing their identity to some shape-shifting profit-centric organisation. If they were to sign, they said, they demanded complete control of all band-related activity, including graphic and stylistic rights. Eventually, in October 1980, the band signed to Chrysalis and the ruffed, frilly shirt was allowed to run free. 'Musclebound', the group's breakthrough hit, saw them looking like Beau Brummel's idea of Braveheart. Tony Hadley was to eventually favour evening dress,

including black tie and cummerbund, but for 'Musclebound' he wore big, billowing sleeves with a large strip of silky material draped over one shoulder, as though he had been caught shopping for curtain fabric. The cissy side of rock had come out of the closet.

Not since the end of the Fifties, and Cliff Richard's inspired fad for black shirts and thin white ties – a look developed by the unlikely red-shirted likes of Kraftwerk and one Cliff was wearing until the Eighties – had the shirt been so pre-eminent in rock 'n' roll imagery. Everything after New Romanticism looked dull, as if it lacked effort. The Cure's Robert Smith made an almost anti-fashion

statement with oversized, non-descript and inevitably black shirts – presumably his dressing-up alternative to the oversized sweater – while Michael Jackson attempted some glamour by adding epaulettes to his. But by the Nineties rock had given up on shirts. The grunge set of Pearl Jam and Nirvana emulated Neil Young by wearing checked lumberjack shirts, which became essential grunge fan kit, and Oasis polished it off with their ordinary, ladsy untucked styles.

Neil Young, music and style guru to the grunge generation

But if the New Romantics made something of their shirts, perhaps its love of the kilt – a garment that Jean-Paul Gaultier attempted to revive in the late Eighties – was an admission that trousers were not really its field. Gary Kemp had a habit of wearing Bowie-style baggy, multi-pleated pairs with braces, forgetting to wear a shirt at all (had Tony taken them all?). But rock trews never recovered from punk.

Queen's Freddie Mercury in his trademark leotard

Just as after New Romanticism all shirts looked safe, so after punk, did trousers. Few acts were able to make a such an impression on the public with their trousers. The early Eighties saw the Jam at the height of their appeal giving a boost to the Mod look, this time among suburban US teens, who suddenly took to neat, dark trousers, parkas and multi-mirrored scooters. Another revival occurred in the summer of 1995, but this time was a more mainstream affair – inspired by the Sixties-influenced English indie band wave of Blur, Supergrass and Menswear, but emanating from the studios of Prada, Gucci and Calvin Klein rather than from the street.

The key events in trouser development post-punk were altogether more embarrassing. Freddy Mercury's leotard-cum-jumpsuit thankfully never made it beyond the stage. Bros' ripped denim harked back to The Ramones and punk, but lacked the punkish free-form approach to style. Self-consciously marketable, Bros trousers became the dress code for a million teenage girls and led to wholesale destruction of countless pairs of Levi 501s –

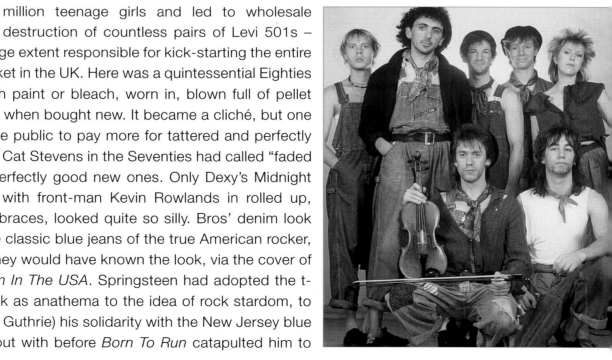

Five years before grunge, Dexy's Midnight Runners model the dirt-poor farmer look

indeed, they were to a large extent responsible for kick-starting the entire second-hand denim market in the UK. Here was a quintessential Eighties look: jeans splashed with paint or bleach, worn in, blown full of pellet holes, already old friends when bought new. It became a cliché, but one that encouraged a gullible public to pay more for tattered and perfectly faded jeans – a style that Cat Stevens in the Seventies had called "faded out to the sky" – than perfectly good new ones. Only Dexy's Midnight Runners' gypsy period, with front-man Kevin Rowlands in rolled up, cropped denim bib-and-braces, looked quite so silly. Bros' denim look was almost a take on the classic blue jeans of the true American rocker, Eddie Cochran – or, as they would have known the look, via the cover of Bruce Springsteen's *Born In The USA*. Springsteen had adopted the t-shirt and faded jeans look as anathema to the idea of rock stardom, to demonstrate (a la Woody Guthrie) his solidarity with the New Jersey blue collar workers he hung out with before *Born To Run* catapulted him to

"Part of the Levi's marketing policy is to place product with varied artists, both mainstream and niche. Each artist is carefully considered before deciding on which product, mainline or capsule, is relevant, and how this is relayed to the consumer. The agreement works both ways. Sometimes we approach them, depending on the artists' plans in relation to our marketing strategy.

"We have worked with Jamiroquai (who we custom make product for) and Massive Attack from very early on in their music careers. Other artists who wear our product are Oasis, Robbie Williams, All Saints, Headswim, AIR, Ocean Colour Scene, Terrorvision, Paul Weller, Spiritualised, Lo-Fi Allstars, Death in Vegas, Boyzone, Hurricane No1, Roni Size, Finlay Quaye, Goldie, Metalheadz and David Bowie."

Michael Chetcuti marketing projects co-ordinator, Levi's

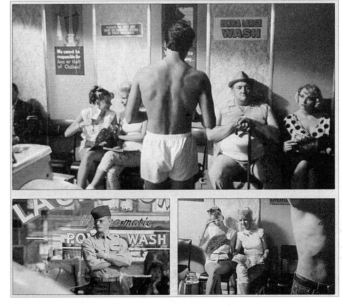

Scenes from Levi's innovative 501 ad featuring Nick Kamen

Facing page: The Goss Bros in matching tears

James Brown in the mid-1970s. GFOS stands for Godfather Of Soul

Sly Stone: the true style god of funk

Scenes from the rock wardrobe: L-R Mel B's vinyl suit from Spiceworld: The Movie, 1997

Now known as Chef from South Park, Isaac Hayes was a fashion Don in the early 1970s. A man so sure of his masculinity that he could wear girly shoes and carry a handbag

megastardom in 1975. Not that anyone cared by the late Eighties. Levis had domination of the world jeans market and played their rock heritage for all it was worth; a series of clever ads teamed classic Sixties soul and rock songs with their brand, suggesting that Levis had helped invent the whole genre. One of the most successful ads used Marvin Gaye's 'Heard It Through The Grapevine'. The

I wanna be adored: The Stone Roses in second generation flared jeans

song had been a hit in 1969 when Marvin was undoubtedly the best-dressed soul man around – and wouldn't be seen dead in denim.

In the Nineties, it has been argued that one trouser style came from music to dominate the broad fashion scene: the combat pant. The trend was driven by rappers reworking the Yippies opposing US intervention in Vietnam and The Clash's ironic fashion statement, with acts such as the Wu-Tang Clan and The Fugees, among others, donning combats to stress the point that it was a jungle out there, and they were fighting the system ad nauseum.

Certainly, hip-hop style has influenced mainstream fashion to make utilitywear everyday garments. The relationship between this musical genre and streetwear became almost symbiotic by the end of the Nineties – bands launched their own fashion brands (such as The Beastie Boys' Mike Diamond's X-Large label), and new streetwear brands were given support by the stars: FUBU, a brand launched in the early Nineties, for instance, was used in an LL Cool J video, as well as being worn by the likes of Mariah Carey, Mary J. Blige, Boyz II Men and Snoop Doggy Dog – just as, in the Eighties, Run DMC popularised adidas trainers with fat (if not phat) laces and LL Cool J started a trend for Kangol hats and Timberland boots.

All Saints model late-1990s urban guerrilla chic

But how the great have fallen: combats followed a downward path from the hardcore black militia look of Public Enemy, preaching the threat of race war against injustice and biased media hype, to the softcore pouting of All Saints, teaching little girls how to love their boyfriends and little boys how to spend too much time alone in their bedrooms.

Not that the trend for combat trousers and utility sportswear by all strands of the music business shows any signs of abating. Increasingly the trend for both stage and street wear has been toward a macho unisex image which leaves male performers with little option but to strip off their shirts altogether to attempt to make an impression on fickle fans and demonstrate their virility. Like The Red Hot Chili Peppers in the Eighties, acts such as Dru Hill have taken to stripping off shirts (although not trousers in Dru's case) to garner media coverage. By the end of the Nineties, it had become very rare to see a man on stage wearing both trousers and a shirt.

Keith Richard in Brooks Brothers-style, round collared, small check shirt circa 1964

The Monkees in cavalry-inspired shirts, hipster boot-cut flares and groovy Cuban-heeled Beatle boots

dresses|skirts

Connie Francis
in a slightly
less demure
pedal-pusher
trouser suit than
was the norm for
the late 1950s

Rock 'n' roll, being the musical embodiment of teenage adolescence, was always naturally confused about sexuality. Elvis excited not just women, but young men, too (not that the fact was readily admitted). He dressed in a (for the time) curiously feminine manner; pink shirts, long hair and jewellery, his lipsticked full-pouting lips in a constant sneer. And he always got the girls. From the beginning, the lyrics of rock embodied masculine teen ideals: getting the girl/car/money. Women, like cars, were objects of desire only, and the latter appeared easier to acquire.

Until the end of the Fifties there really were no great female rock 'n' roll singers. Country singers like Brenda Lee or Wanda Jackson could belt out a Western-influenced R&B tune, and former Doris Day sound-alike Connie Francis developed an MOR rock market, but there wasn't a rock-born female star who hadn't enjoyed a career in another musical field prior to crossing over into the rock market. The women who had been drafted into the rock 'n' roll revolution up until 1959, coming from the more staid pop and country areas, all dressed in the regular female fashions of the

The First Female
Sex Symbol of
rock 'n' roll:
Jayne Mansfield

day; jeans and sweaters, calf-length dresses, multi-petticoated skirts that twirled when they danced, hair usually in either a ponytail or in a teased and set style which still had echoes of the Forties.

It's telling that the first woman to be strongly identified with rock 'n' roll was a film star. Jayne Mansfield, in *The Girl Can't Help It* (1956) provided the filler between set numbers from Little Richard, Fats Domino and Gene Vincent, among others. Shaped like every cartoonist's dream, she bulged in all the right places to set males pulses racing, and was perfect as the a dumb blonde who,

Working girls: The Supremes step out in – for them – unusually plain two-piece suits

with the help of a scheming PR man, becomes a rock 'n' roll star. Which was remarkably prescient of director Frank Taschlin (who also made the withering *Will Success Spoil Rock Hunter?*).

With the dawning of the second decade of rock 'n' roll came the first wave of female singers who hadn't had any other career. In America it was the soul boom which came out of the major industrial cities of the North that threw up a whole bunch of female stars, primarily in all-

Tina Turner out-shimmies her Ikettes

girl groups: The Crystals, The Shirelles, The Exciters (who included one male member), Ronnie Spector and The Ronettes, The Shangri-Las, Tina Turner And The Ikettes and the undisputed queens of teen scream, The Supremes. That each of these groups had a male mentor meant little except that the clothes they wore and the image they all projected were calculated to excite the boys and impress the girls who watched them perform and bought their records.

Ike Turner, husband to Tina, was an old hand at the music business by the time he and Tina scored a minor hit in 1960 with 'A Fool In Love'. He understood that boys and men liked to watch women dressed none-too demurely belting out R&B grooves. Tina must have liked it, too. Although at the start she wore the high hair and knee-length two-piece suits which were de rigueur for the time, Ike

Inventing sex appeal: Ronnie Spector (centre) and The Ronettes

Ike and Tina Turner in smart daywear, distinctly more sober and less revealing than their work clothes

soon had her in glittering mini-dresses in contrast to The Ikettes in their all-white trouser suits, faux sailor dresses and so on. Tina Turner could wear a skirt as though it was an offensive weapon, a short concoction of tassel and sequins that shimmered when she shimmied, transmitting an eat-men-for-breakfast carnality that left you in no doubt as to who was in control. It's a look that served her well and which she's refused to give up well into the Nineties.

Phil Spector, although much younger than Ike Turner, had no less stringent views on what his girl groups should wear, how they should dance and what they should sing. Like Ike, he married his leading lady, 20-year-old Ronnie Bennett, but unlike Ike, he'd already scored million-sellers with a previous all-girl group, The Crystals. With the Ronettes Spector, famously employing his Wall Of Sound recording technique, created a far more physical phenomenon. All three Ronettes wore high hair, heavy eyelashes with tight skirt and jacket suits or single, sleeveless dresses which emphasised their curves and stopped just short of the knee, giving full view of either fetishistically sharp winkle-picker stilettos, or knee-high, calf-hugging leather boots. With the combination of Ronnie's tremulous voice the epic, reverb-laden backing (with voices sometimes added by Cher) and freshly post-pubescent girls snaking their hips to the beat, The Ronettes brought a female sexuality to rock 'n' roll that was, briefly, the equal of Elvis and The Beatles.

Ronnie Spector on the comeback trail (1977), demonstrating the charms that appealed to Phil Spector fifteen years earlier

At the same time that The Ronettes were sexing up the music business, Berry Gordy Junior's Supremes were adding glamour and sophistication to the soul scene, in the process starting a trend among middle-class white America (and Britain) for wearing evening gowns. The Supremes wore stage clothes, as did their male counterparts The Temptations and Four Tops. Diana Ross, Mary Wilson and Florence Ballard would don sculptured wigs, heavy false eyelashes and either floor-length evening gowns or Chanel-inspired two-piece suits to take to the stage. The Supremes' sexuality was far less raw than The Ronettes, it was more adult but no less obvious. Just as the pencil skirts and stilettos matched Ronnie Spector's voice, so the elegant lines of their backless gowns matched Diana Ross' velvet tones.

In the UK, Brian Epstein, who had so successfully capitalised on the inherent sex appeal of four working-class lads from Liverpool, fell into a close friendship with the cloakroom girl at the Cavern Club. He decided that he could make her a star, too. Priscilla

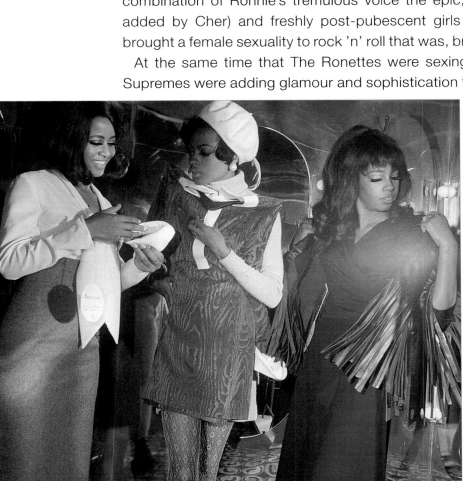

Diana Ross and The Supremes trying out London fashions, 1968

CILLA

Cilla (before the nose job) showing off her girl-next-door homely appeal

White changed her name to the more threatening Cilla Black and, wearing knee-length dresses, her red hair in a semi-Cleopatra cut and a voice as tremulous as Ronnie Spector's, became a pop star – but not a sex symbol. She had an unthreatening, girl-next-door appeal which worked in terms of record sales (and later transferred to a hugely successful television career). Likewise her skirts and dresses were the stuff of High Street windows across the country.

Cilla didn't exactly blaze a trail for female singers in Britain. Before her Dusty Springfield had, with a pure, soulful voice and the largest amount of eye kohl ever seen on one woman, become a star. Dusty wasn't exactly a fashion icon, in fact she looked more like a teenage girl's mother than the teen, but her bouffant 'Beehive' hairdo – a style borrowed from The Ronettes – was at the time *the* High Street style to have, and she wore the more demure fashions of the day. In 1964 the 16-year-old Lulu became an instant star when her version of The Isley Brothers' 'Shout' demonstrated not just her impressive lung power but also her skill at shaking her thing in a Mary Quant mini-skirt.

In the mid-Sixties, the rock business truly came to terms with the fact that sex appeal was as big a part of a female singer's success as ability. Not that many of the singers who made it had little talent.

Dusty Springfield looking older, in 1964, than she did ten years later

Little Lulu attemps a Jayne Mansfield pose

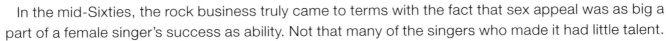

Fashion queen Mary Quant styling the new look at her Carnaby Street boutique, circa 1966

"In 1955... Mary Quant opened a shop called Bazaar on the King's Road, based on the kind of clothes that art students were wearing and, straightaway, she turned the whole of women's fashion upside down."

Nik Cohn

Your mother would like it... twistin' the evening away, before the mini-skirt

"Courreges, Mary Quant and Vidal Sassoon. Scientific precision, mathematical beauty resulting in a rhythm of life, allowing youth to de-drab for the first time since the Twenties and wear its masculinity and femininity to the advantage of both. Thus style begot realisation, attitude and a firm advertisement for where we were going."

Andrew Loog Oldham

Sandie Shaw, for instance, was a fine singer who just happened to have stunning cheekbones, fine, straight hair and long, slender legs which were never encumbered by shoes. Shoes, or rather lack of them, were Sandie's gimmick. Not that she needed one. She scored a string of hit singles which reached a sales peak (and artistic nadir) in 1969 with 'Puppet On A String'. By which time Sandie had met many clothes designers and opened her own boutique selling the kind of flowery dresses and mini-skirts for which she was famous.

Proof that sex appeal could outsell talent came in 1965 when Sonny And Cher scored a world-wide hit single with 'I Got You Babe'. A terrible song of schmaltzy sentimentality, Cher's voice carried half the tune and her stunning looks and furry hippy clothes carried the rest. While husband Sonny Bono looked ridiculous in the clothes they wore, she always looked gorgeous, even before plastic surgery.

As Sonny and Cher became famous, they introduced a West Coast fashion trend to the world.

Nobody had used the term unisex very much until 1966, much like nobody had used the terms Acid, love-in or love and peace, man. After The Beatles gave Hippy the seal of approval, everyone talked the talk and dressed the dress, of course. John Lennon and Yoko Ono both wore kimonos and north African dhotis in public, Mick Jagger and his then current companion Marianne Faithfull both appeared in velvet suits with ruffle-fronted shirts, equally long hair and high-heeled boots. Donovan summed things up perfectly (if a little late) when he sang "Is it a boy or is it

a girl, takes all kinds to make the world go round."

Unisex proved to be the real sexual revolution of the Sixties. Men's hair was getting longer, women were wearing trousers – mostly jeans – and couples were slipping into whatever their partner had left lying around the night before. In America, Joni

Mitchell and Janis Joplin demonstrated a musical ability without exploiting their sexuality in the obvious way. They weren't dressing up in stage clothes or evening wear. Mama Cass and Michelle Phillips of The Mamas And Papas, Cher and Grace Slick all dressed in clothes that they felt comfortable in, clothes which would then be worn on Haight Ashbury.

By the end of the Sixties, 'serious' female artists didn't wear dresses as a means of reflecting their femininity, even to deflect attention away from the rough, combative nature of many of their songs. The dress was camouflage for the urban subversive of the time, it wasn't about anything as trivial as fashion. With the politicisation of rock, fashion apparently became irrelevant. Clothes were worn by rock stars as statements of where their head was at (man). Which is why Mick Jagger chose a Michael Fish dress to appear at the Stones' Hyde Park gig in 1969. Given the fact that Stones

Mick Jagger in Michael Fish frock at Hyde Park concert, 1969

"I'd been hassled to go to Canada with the London/English look ('the Brits are coming') and I had to miss Prince Rupert Lowenstein's White Ball at his house. So I was away having a horrible time, but Mick went into (my shop) Mr Fish to get a white outfit for the ball.

"I'd made two outfits, one in purple and one in white, for a fashion show at the London Planetarium. One was made for Calvin Lockhart, this most beautiful black actor, and one for Lord Lichfield. The trousers and gillet were moiré, without sleeves. I'd been to Greece for a holiday, and the silhouette that stuck in my mind, which was never seen in this country, was on the soldiers where this extraordinary thing stuck up at the sides and had pom poms. I thought 'My God! If anyone in England wore that – imagine.'

"So I told my designer what I wanted. When it was done, Barry Sainsbury put Patrick (Lichfield) off, saying 'You'll look like a big girl's blouse wearing that.' Calvin Lockheart also went wobbly. The boy who wore it was a very sweet Scottish shepherd called Stuart. So there was this one white outfit and the purple one (I'd love to know where the purple one is) and in came Mick when I was away and picked it up and probably said, 'Can I have it cheap, because it's been worn?' and 'Put it on my account' probably, because he's always rather careful. Nothing wrong with being careful.

"The first thing I knew about it was when I came back on the aeroplane from Canada (feeling fucked, really, in every possible way. Ripped off, travel weary) to see a front page: 'Where Did You Get That Frock?' Going on, 'You can get this frock from Sheila in the King's Road.' A line for line copy. Already. Well, I nearly died. You could have knocked me down with a feather.

"Most people think that Ozzie Clark made that outfit, because he was backstage at the gig, and had helped Mick put all the butterflies in the box the night before. Ozzie and I used to laugh about it. He used to say, 'Michael, I'm always telling people it's nothing to do with me'."

Michael Fish

Mick and Marianne swap wardrobe secrets

American hippies show how to just let it all hang out, maaaan

founder member Brian Jones had died two days earlier, one might have expected Jagger to wear black or for the gig to be cancelled. No such thing occurred. This was to be a ground-breaking event, expected to have a major effect on both his band's career and the rock business in general. By wearing what was essentially a white moiré mini-dress over white trousers (which its designer had based on the uniform of the Greek National Guard), Jagger, his lips smeared with blood-red lipstick, his hair newly washed and hanging over his shoulders, gave a performance of unprecedented sexual ambiguity. It was a theme he would explore famously on film in *Performance* (again in an Indian inspired 'dress' designed by Michael Fish) and on stage for the next twenty years.

While Jagger's cross-dressing had a minimal direct effect on street fashion, it undoubtedly helped promote the unisex trend. Other male rock stars, however, quickly latched onto the 'dangerous' notion of wearing dresses.

In 1968, David Bowie was just beginning to develop his outrageous stage persona. He'd previously caused a minor incident in 1965 when his hair was almost deemed too long to allow him to appear on television, but had thus far failed to score a big hit. Always a man with an eye for the cutting edge, Bowie quickly latched on to the appeal of androgyny and before developing the extraterrestrial (and ambisexual) Ziggy Stardust, caused a furore in ultra-conservative Texas and even Los Angeles when, in 1971, he walked the streets wearing dresses. Bowie further capitalised on the furore when he attempted to release an album, *The Man Who Sold The World*, with a cover that showed him lounging on a chaise wearing a dress. A reporter asked him why he was wearing it. "You must understand that it's not a woman's dress. It's a man's dress," Bowie replied. It was, in fact, another of Michael Fish's designs.

Who's that girl?: The controversial The Man Who Sold The World album sleeve

"The important fact is that don't have to drag up," Bowie added. 'I'm just a cosmic yob, I suppose. I've always worn my own style of clothes. I design them. I just don't like the clothes that you buy in shops. I don't wear dresses all the time, either. I change every day. I'm not outrageous. I'm David Bowie."

Establishing an identity was of paramount importance of any rock star then. The early Seventies was a time of great flux in both the rock and fashion worlds. For the first time in its history, rock suffered a revival of an earlier form, Fifties rock 'n' roll, a hitherto unheardof event but one which would become a regular recurrence in the development of popular music. Chuck Berry scored his first number one single with a reworking of a 1952 Dave Bartholomew R&B novelty song, 'My Ding-A-Ling', while The Drifters and Elvis found themselves once again topping the charts on both sides of the Atlantic. The fashion world, meanwhile, was busy reinventing the Twenties and Thirties; Biba brought back the cloche hat, flapper dresses, feather boas and platforms. Glam rock in the States was pioneered by The New York Dolls and Iggy Pop, both of whom proudly wore dresses and slut-make up. In the UK top glam acts Slade and Sweet

Model outside the ineffably elegant Biba shop, London

The archetypal hippy chick: Stevie Nicks before being influenced by the Good Witch of the North

Christine McVie in medieval-style rock chick frock

had one member who'd wear floor-length coats that doubled as dresses with apparent pride. All while women in the music business seemed to be shunning dresses in favour of hot pants, jeans, leather trousers or men's suits.

Perhaps because street fashion had decided that skirts and dresses should be midi- or maxi-length, only women on the so-called 'serious' side of the music business (quaintly referred to by men with beards and Army greatcoats as the 'underground' scene) wore them. Fleetwood Mac's twin sisters of surreality, Christine McVie and Stevie Nicks, single-handedly invented the mystic white witch of rock look; lots of layers mixing ancient lace shawls, floor-length skirts, long, wild hair and Indian shirts. It was a look that girlfriends of stoned hippies had to have and in certain parts of America's mid-West and Britain's Eastern counties have retained to this day. How Kate Bush succeeded with a similar look is as mystifying as the appeal of her singing style.

In the mid-Seventies, apart for Diana Ross, who continued to wear evening gowns, more and more female pop stars who were being 'discovered' wore short shorts and tight tops. If women in music

Diana Ross in the mid-1970s

Facing page: The first glam band to champion the big girls' blouse, The New York Dolls

Abba have so many things to answer for. The T-shirt dress and white knee-high boots, to mention but two

aspired to be more 'serious' without being 'underground', they continued in the unisex trend by wearing jeans, leather trousers and suits or more masculine attire, albeit in titillating fashion as perfectly demonstrated by The Runaways (a teenage all-girl wet-dream creation of middle-aged producer Kim Fowley). Frida and Agnetha of Abba became the biggest female names in the business in 1974 when the group won the Eurovision Song Contest performing 'Waterloo', with the result that, when they wore clothes that were even remotely sane enough to be worn in the street, they were copied. From Stockholm to Seattle, Stevenage to Springfield, women wore versions of Abba's jumpsuits, patched jeans, hotpants and A-line denim skirts. Abba founder Bjorn was to remark twenty-five years later that the band had committed "serious crimes against fashion".

Gloria Gaynor shows how to survive gigantic flares

Some aspects of Abba's wear were being copied from the one source of inspiration that had prevailed since the early Sixties. The dance scene had long dictated the street fashion agenda for the hip and truly trendy, and in the Seventies it continued to do so. As discos flourished across the western world, so, too, did disco wear. Singers like Gloria Gaynor, Chaka Khan and Donna Summer sparkled as they sang, sending sales of boob tubes, halter-neck tops and hip-hugging flares soaring. It helped that models, artists, film stars and minor royalty were forever being photographed in various New York and London discos clearly having the time of their lives and dressed in much more expensive but similarly styled disco wear. Mick Jagger and his soon to be ex-wife Bianca were forever appearing in magazines dancing at Studio 54 with Andy, Truman, Grace Jones and various

The first true marraige of rock and fashion: Grace Jones in Issey Miyake

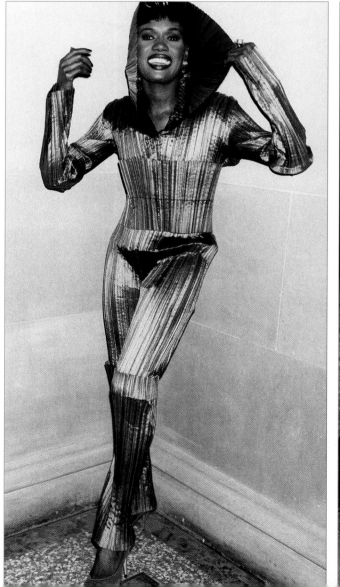

Girls will be boys: Grace in her gender-flipping flat-top and suit

Facing page: Jones was a model, her manager was a fashion photographer (Jean Paul Goude), her records (produced by her record company's owner) were perfect for the fashion runways

New York alumni, Jagger by now in more masculine garb, Bianca always in revealing, slinky dresses, tops and shirts.

As disco decadence and pop pap began to lose their appeal to a new generation of bored teenagers, a new wave of music and fashion was being born. Punk was as much the child of fashion designers as it was 'musicians'. For possibly the first time since Brian Epstein, one man's idea of how his band should look helped to create a whole fashion movement and youth cult.

Malcolm McLaren had dealt in second-hand and retro rock clothing since the early Seventies at his Chelsea shop, originally titled Let It Rock and then Too Fast To Live, Too Young To Die. He'd seen The New York Dolls up close and apparently was deeply jealous of Andy Warhol's Factory scene in New York. Malcolm wanted his own scene full of dangerous characters, musicians, film-makers, poets, artists, models and designers. A born prankster, with the ego and ambition of a nineteenth century industrialist, McLaren had no talent for either performing or designing, but he knew the appeal of shock and helped transport the schlock and roll genre which began with Alice Cooper in the late Sixties and was further subverted by the Dolls' junk culture, to the UK. McLaren, by all accounts a shy and feeble child, was thrilled by the violence and social unrest caused first by Teds, then Mods and finally America's Yippies and the student rebels of Paris in the late Sixties. His obsession with the clothing and music of the Teds reflected this. McLaren's partner, the older and more fashion-experienced Vivienne Westwood, had the references and ability to turn his mad ideas into action in their shops which, by the time punk had really begun, had changed its name to Sex and was selling fetish rubber-wear.

Rip her to shreds: Typical example of DIY punk gear, circa 1976

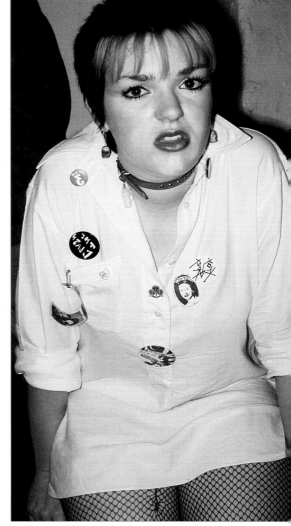

For Westwood, punk was a starting point for a long and hype-filled career in fashion. It was at this time that she first started dressing her willing 'models' (shop girl Jordan, camp followers Sue Catwoman, Chrissie Hynde and others) in underwear as outerwear. Malcolm, of course, recruited his Sex Pistols from the shop's staff (bassist Glen Matlock was a Saturday boy) and customers (Rotten would wander around sneering at the prices, Cook and Jones would try to steal whatever they could).

As the street punk style developed, articles of conformist clothing were, out of necessity, parodied and re-invented. Most punks had neither the access to nor money for McLaren's Chelsea-priced gear. So, across the country boys and girls were raiding their parent's wardrobes for old clobber that they could customise. The feminine symbol of Sixties sexual freedom, the mini-skirt, was worn ripped, scrawled with slogans, re-made out of rubber, leather or tartan, covered with zips and chains and worn over ripped stockings. Siouxsie Sioux, self-styled leader of the Bromley contingent, a bunch of bored lower-middle class suburban teenagers, wore her skirt as battle-dress rather than a means of pulling a fella, emphasising her combative nature by wearing cupless bras and a swastika armband. The female punk look was overtly sexual, mixing

Siouxsie Sioux shows her regrettable penchant for Nazi chic at the Screen On The Green, 1976

Debbie Harry and the rest of the band, late 1970s. Blondie are a band. Right?

fetishistic images with militaristic emblems and layers of war-paint make-up with self-mutilation in the form of safety pins stuck through cheeks, ears and noses.

In America, the female punk look was less design-conscious, but no less sexual. Deborah Harry of Blondie, a former Playboy bunny and psychedelic rock chick, was almost thirty years old when she and her boyfriend's band got their first rave reviews for gigs at CBGBs, the home of New York punk. Blondie played old-fashioned Sixties harmonies, the men in the band wore black two-piece suits with white shirts and skinny ties, but Debbie wore short skirts – with a vengeance. This was the skirt as allure, a feminine counter to the new wave pick'n'mix of punk and retro pop that constituted the band's sound. Prefiguring the dolled-up, lipstick and micro-mini get-up of the women musicians in Robert Palmer's 'Addicted to Love' video, Harry played the bombshell expertly. In rock 'n' roll terms, she reinvented the skirt as something feminine but certainly not soft. She'd wear a ripped and frayed t-shirt as a dress, her clearly-dyed blond mane dishevelled and awry,

Debbie Harry and the rest of the band, late 1990s. Blondie are a band. Right?

Facing page:
Debbie Harry

Not all of the
Harry wardrobe
was a success

Following pages:
*Debbie Harry
demonstrating
how the world
first developed a
love of fake fur
(the dress on
the right looks
suspiciously like
the dreadful
Zandra Rhodes
punk-inspired
couture item
which mocked
the political roots
of the movement)*

Annie Lennox, the first mass-market female gender bender in rock

Patti Smith in PVC trousers and her dad's shirt and waistcoat

her make-up heavy and slightly skewed. Maybe it was her razor-sharp cheekbones, maybe it was her overt sexuality, but, whatever it was, Debbie upset feminists something rotten. Womenswear chain stores loved her, however, and little black dresses, black and white checked mini skirts and t-shirt dresses made their way into shopfronts the world over. None of it bore Debbie or Blondie's name, but all of it bore her imprint.

Debbie Harry created a revolution in the music business. Blondie were both a commercial and critical musical success and had, in the shape of their singer, a credible fashion figure. This was something that, previously, no female-fronted band or solo performer had achieved. Harry's female contemporaries Patti Smith and Siouxsie Sioux enjoyed more limited commercial success and had far less influence over popular fashion. Patti Smith was undoubtedly credible both musically and artistically, but her only hit single was a cover version of a Bruce Springsteen song and, try as she might, she simply wasn't a sexually alluring feminine figure to the mass market, despite Robert Mapplethorpe's best efforts to transform her into an icon. Wearing a man's suit on the cover of her first album, *Horses,* was not such a great gimmick, either, given that loveable little Lulu had, the year previously, scored a world-wide hit single with David Bowie's 'The Man Who Sold The World' (clearly the cross-dressers anthem) dressed as a man, in a pinstripe three-piece suit, white tie and fedora. Strangely, perhaps, only one other

Lulu performing Bowie's 'The Man Who Sold The World.' When he recorded it, he wore a dress...

Facing page: Eurythmics' Annie Lennox in Blade Runner-inspired make-up

"Jean-Paul Gaultier saved her career with that corset."

Tom Gilby

Above left:
*Debbie Harry
does Mae West*

Above centre:
*The Gaultier
corset which kept
her act together*

Above right:
*Madonna (as
Jean Harlow)
with Gaultier
(as himself)*

female artist successfully managed an androgynous image: Annie Lennox. The combination of her shock of hair, strong jaw-line and ability to appear sexy to heterosexuals while dressed as a man was unique. It was a talent she continued to exploit until deciding that Mickey Mouse ears were a better gimmick and ended up looking as mad as a hatter while performing 1996's 'No More I Love Yous'.

Siouxsie Sioux eventually became a Goth grandmother, her appeal proving to have durable niche value, but no real mainstream potential. Hers was a cartoon look, her fussy, black fancy dress of interest to those troubled teenagers who hadn't quite got over the fact that everyone dies, although probably not for a few decades. Aspects of all three women's styles were distinctive and of merit, however, and they were soon to be assimilated into the wardrobe of rock's first true female superstar.

Madonna took Siouxsie's lace, leather and layers, Smith's attitude and androgyny (over-sized man's jacket) and Debbie Harry's hair, eye make-up, and appropriated her sexuality in order to configure the first 'Holiday' era look. By wearing her skirt

*Britain's own
Breakfast Bunch
poop femmes
Banarama*

"Madonna has been the top influence everywhere. She popularised the bustier fashion look. Then the Truck Driver Tank Top look with fashionable pumping iron shoulders which everyone now has. She has created fashion for grown-ups with the Japanese Geisha look – white face make-up, long straight black hair, kimono dress and platform boots."

Mary Quant

over leggings, in a manner suggestive of both Harry and Siouxsie, she 'invented' a style imitated by Bananarama and, subsequently, street style in the UK and USA (at the time, Madonna's leggings were only matched in popularity by Toni Basil's ra-ra skirt in which she so cutely twirled while intoning 'Hey Mickey' over and over).

Over the next decade, Madonna would sample different aspects of all three women's wardrobes, mixing them with items from the styles of Marilyn Monroe, Jayne Mansfield and even Mae West in her ever-changing look until the day that she took her dress and made it transparent, by (shades of Siouxsie) wearing her underwear as outerwear. After the PR disaster that was *Sex* the book, French couturier Jean-Paul Gaultier put Madonna in a conical bra for her Blonde Ambition tour in 1990, and saved her career. Curiously, while Gaultier also succeed in making the pin-

Facing page:
*The Witches Of
Candlewick –
Madonna,
Donatella Versace
and Cher*

stripe suit acceptable clubwear (largely via Madonna again), he spent many subsequent seasons trying – and failing – to get men into skirts.

Madonna's collaboration with Gaultier set another precedent. Afterwards, it became the norm for 'name' designers to be associated with rock stars, either by having them model for them, or simply supplying them with clothes. The outfits would then be mentioned in the first paragraph of any interview the star would do with a style-obsessed Eighties press. Her obvious delight at finding a new avenue of exploitation for rock was reflected in the writing and recording of 'Vogue', in the video for which she attempted to look like the supermodels who were stealing her media coverage at the time. The song and video abjectly failed to start a dance trend which, although hyped by an eager press, only made dance crowds (famously – and snobbishly – exclusive) snort with derision.

It's almost impossible to tell if Madonna materially affected the design and fashion obsessions of the Eighties, if she simply followed in their wake and was a product of them, or whether it was a matter of right time, right place. There's no doubt that her choice of clothing for videos (excepting the truly outrageous ones) were often not simply costumes, but were 'real' items that could be bought, or cheaper copies of them could be bought, in most shopping malls.

Possibly because most of Madonna's looks were retro-based, and the world felt that it had seen everything by that time (and anyone who'd bought *Sex* certainly saw everything Madonna had to offer), she failed to have as big an impact on street style as Debbie Harry had. Certainly, Madonna's hardcore fans across the globe (in 1987 there were a lot of them) tended to dress just like her, but they were not truly discerning when it came to sartorial matters. Even after she had dismissed them as Wannabes, they continued to ape her dress, and embarrass her by doing so.

By the early Nineties, Madonna was in search of musical credibility and playing down her fashion obsession. After the 1991 film *In Bed With Madonna* had revealed just a little too much of her vain, sometimes cruel posturings, her record sales slipped,

The First Couple
of grunge

Kurt Cobain, in touch with his feminine side

her film appearances were routinely mocked and her confused philosophy of life was not so eagerly sought. By the end of the decade she attempted another reinvention, wearing the clothes of a wealthy forty-year old mother, which was just what she was. She also employed the services of British dance producer William Orbit to inject some credibility into her voice. It seemed to work.

As Madonna was starting to lose popular support in the early Nineties, however, a new musical and fashion movement was just emerging from rain-soaked Seattle. Grunge, the music and attitude, was little more than a belated case of UK punk finding voice in bored provincial teenagers. Figurehead Kurt Cobain of Nirvana, a clearly mixed-up kid from a classically dysfunctional family, found a soulmate in the equally mixed-up kid from a weirdly dysfunctional family, Courtney Love. They shared everything together, including her punk-inspired, second-hand ripped dresses.

Cobain was making a point by wearing them – whether it was his or Courtney's point is hard to tell – that being, he was in touch with his feminine side, and/or confused about his identity and who wore the pants in their family. As crass as it sounds, Cobain's behaviour was indicative of a social malaise affecting a large part of western civilisation; because of changing social patterns, men's role in life was becoming unsure, more and more families were dependent upon one (predominantly female) parent. Cobain, like a whole generation of kids born in the late Sixties and early Seventies, was from a broken home and had no father figure to impress upon him the rules of how to act like a man. Not that any such realisation explained why other rockers and fans took to wearing dresses; grunge pin-up Evan Dando, of The Lemonheads, took to fame like a duck to an oil-slick and began taking lots of drugs and wearing his (many) girlfriends' dresses. He did so in order to both show a solidarity with Cobain and impress the girls that he was in touch with his feminine side. Various Red Hot Chili Peppers did so as a brazen invitation for rednecks to challenge their machismo, while The Butthole Surfers cross-dressed as a crass statement about their sexuality.

Cobain was not cross-dressing to shock in the same way that Bowie had done twenty years earlier, although in yet another bizarre link back to *The Man Who Sold The World*, Cobain had been playing the song since he was a teenager, and Nirvana would, before his suicide, cover it. Cobain's fate is not

Original riot grrrls The Slits

the only reason why images of him in women's wear are far more disturbing than those of Bowie. The fact that the American had no real understanding of why he was doing it other than feeling driven to is far more unsettling.

For many (male) conspiracy theorists and misogynists, Courtney Love became a figure of blame and hate following her husband's suicide. Like only Yoko Ono before her, she had to put up with the uninformed and generally uneducated pointing an accusatory finger. It didn't help, of course, that Love's image was one step beyond Debbie Harry; all smudged make-up, ripped baby-doll dresses, big boots, dark roots and swearing.

Love and her female contemporaries were part of a new post-feminist movement that knew what they didn't want, and that they didn't want it now. The late Eighties and Nineties spawned a bunch of all-female hardcore rock

The Slits, punk's first and foremost all-female band

groups – among them The Lunachicks, L7, Babes In Toyland and countless riot grrrl groups born of the indie-rock communities in Olympia and Washington in the US – who used a typically male genre to vent a particularly female rage. Courtney named her band Hole after the slang for female genitalia, and in honour of the only previous all-female band who'd shown a mixture of aggravating attitude

PJ Harvey does things her way

and sexuality powered by limited musicianship dressed in Victorian urchin chic, The Slits. Not long after Nirvana's *Nevermind* had gone platinum several times, checked lumberjack shirts, pre-ripped jeans and woolly beanie hats swamped both male and female clothing stores across the globe. Quickly following Love's appearance in a (second-hand) silk nightgown worn as evening wear at a major rock festival, chainstores began selling brand new ones. Instead of subverting their sexuality in the way that Bowie had, Love and her contemporaries chose to twist masculine preconceptions of femininity. By wearing dress styles that mirrored the innocence of childhood – daisy prints, gingham, lacy frills and so on – and being overtly sexually aggressive in manner (Love was forever flashing her breasts at audiences to get a reaction), the riot grrrl movement rebuked the earlier feminist movement's espousal of non-sensual politics. Andrea Dworkin's overalls never had the effect of Sinead O'Connor's shaven head and doe eyes.

Shirley Manson of Garbage in punk-meets-Blade Runner garb

In the wake of the guitar-driven grunge sisters, a new wave of female acts emerged with a look that was neither new nor revolutionary. Their concern was not to shock because of how they looked, but rather how they sounded. PJ Harvey may have appeared on the cover of *Rolling Stone* in her underwear but as the charts blossomed with new female acts, all lyrically forthright, if not darned angry – among them Alanis Morisette, Garbage's Shirley Manson, Elastica's Justine Frischman and No Doubt's Gwen Stefani – there was one thing for sure. There were few dresses in sight. Fashion, indeed, seemed off the menu. Stefani was said to have struck a blow for women in wearing tight, punky trousers and a cropped T-shirt and not worrying about her slight paunch.

Salt-N-Pepa in old skool hip hop wear

On the dance scene, young soul sisters either dressed up in long, expensive sophisticated dresses (like M People's Heather Small) or continued in the style of the few successful female rappers such as Salt-N-Pepa, Yo-Yo and Queen Latifah, who modelled the female versions of sports labelwear that their male counterparts had made so hip; Stussy, Nike, adidas, etc. Mary J Blige took Madonna's overt sexuality to a new level without resorting to Hollywood-inspired fashion clichés, choosing instead to wear in her various videos the current hip labels of the street, both male and female, as well as revealing short dresses, shorts and jumpsuits. Lauryn Hill of The Fugees took a similar route without revealing too much flesh, choosing social politics as a message rather than sexual (as Blige), a mock-militaristic look as stage wear, mixing it with the urban guerrilla gear of rappers – all hooded Stone Island parkas, Air Jordans and combat trousers. For the cover of her multi-million

Lauryn Hill of The Fugees

Lauryn Hill not of The Fugees

Facing page: Alanis Morrisette; much more interested in her work than her image

selling début solo album *The Miseducation Of Lauryn Hill*, the singer discarded the military look in favour of an expensive-looking white, strappy slip dress. Hill's fiercely defended image was one of a strong, independent woman in charge of her life and destiny, rapping to the unconverted, eschewing overt sexuality in favour of a more difficult choice: selling her music, not her body. Not that she rejected materialism altogether; one 1999 interviewer spotted no less than seven items of exclusive Louis Vuitton luggage being taken into her hotel room.

As female rock stars emerged who were not 'sold' by their sexuality, and gave off very serious signals – none more so than Skunk Anansie's lead singer Skin, who shaved her head and wore big boots with combat trousers on stage and showed little sign of Sinead O'Connor's doe-eyed vulnerability – a perverse new pop phenomenon occurred which could almost have been a sub-plot of *The Girl Can't Help It*.

The Spice Girls were possibly rock's last great invention. They were put together by a male manager, Simon Fuller (he also managed Annie Lennox), whose idea it was that five individual female characters with such clearly defined roles that they didn't need proper

Hip hop fashion statement No.9: Cleopatra in snow gear

names, just descriptive monikers – Sporty Spice, Ginger Spice, Scary Spice, Posh Spice and Baby Spice – could clean up in the music market. He was right, of course. But, crucially, he was also wrong. The traditional audience for an act of this kind, adolescent girls, merely laughed at the idea of a five women spouting a Girl Power, pro-feminist manifesto who didn't even have real names. They might have quite liked the Spices' first single 'Tell Me What You Want', but they were far too cynical to fall for such obvious marketing. However, their pre-teen sisters swallowed it whole. The Spice Girls were probably the first instance in the history of rock where parents bought the records, videos, clothes, dolls, spaghetti shapes and magazines on behalf of the real consumer, who was too young to know what pocket money was. The Spice Girls were originally dressed in best high street style to show solidarity with the 11-to-15-year-old girls who also tottered along on inelegant platforms, their puppy-fat thighs wobbling, but they continued to dress in this manner even after their first burst of success because fashion innovation was beyond the imagination and financial restrictions of their core audience. Only ex-Ginger Spice Geri Halliwell proved a force in fashion invention with her Union Jack dress, which prompted the use of the Jack on a range of garments from shoes to underwear and prompted a million imitations at a million tiny tots fancy dress parties. She sold the real article (which had been made by her sister) for a children's charity, appropriately enough, at a Sotheby's auction of pop memorabilia in 1998. It fetched the largest price for a single item that day: $69,000.

In the wake of the Spices, a thousand imitation all-girl groups sprung up, each as desperate to get the same sales as the Spice Girls, but none of them quite managed it. This is undoubtedly because little girls change their minds about what they like faster than Madonna changes her hair. The first

Following pages: Great Britain's Geri Spice in home-made dress and Iceland's Bjork in designer wear.

Facing page:
*All Saint's before
combats fatigue
had set in*

"Now that we're all so clued up about these things, and so knowing about how the media operates, and aware of the role of stylists, the connection between music and fashion is maybe not so powerful. The fashion/music connection is evident everywhere, not least in advertising – it's more visible but maybe it's less potent as a result."

Simon Jordan of Magic Hat

"Bands still have a big influence on the brands and styles worn. But they don't create particular looks anymore. Bewitched wear stage clothes and won't have any influence on fashion. All Saints would probably dress the way they do whether pop stars or not. But in doing so publicly they extend that look."

Nick Logan

British girl band to emerge in their wake actually captured an older audience by virtue of the fact that they had real names and personalities, didn't spout political clichés and sounded like the 'dangerous' R&B bands coming out of the US.

All Saints had more of an eye for trousers than skirts or dresses and were more at ease in Maharishi combat trousers than anything cute. Their dress sense was urban, comfortable, accessible, girlie but not push-over girlie.

Forty-four years after Jayne Mansfield first sashayed into sight in *The Girl Can't Help It*, there are infinitely more women rock stars on show. A lot of them adhere to a marketing man's idea of how they should look, but not all. More than thirty years after her first hit, Cher shared chart space with a bunch of almost identical twenty-something sisters, The Corrs, and their version of a twenty-year-old Fleetwood Mac song. In the videos for their respective songs Cher, dressed in a shorts and t-shirt ensemble, danced at a rave, surrounded by people young enough to be her children. In theirs, The Corrs gazed wistfully at the camera as they played their flutes and fiddles, wearing long, black, floating dresses that their mother would wear. A few weeks later, Debbie Harry was back in the

It's a family affair: David, Zowie (now simply Joe) and Angie Bowie in the early 1970s

BLONDE date

FUSING ROCK, POP, DISCO AND RAP, BLONDIE WERE THE BIGGEST AND MOST INFLUENTIAL BAND OF THEIR TIME. THE BUBBLE BURST IN 1982, BUT NOW THEY'RE BACK. HOWARD WILMOT FINDS OUT WHY...

Following pages: Sharon (left) and Caroline Corrs in simple, if anonymous, chic

Debbie Harry, at 52 still a fashion and sex symbol

Bow Wow Wow's Annabel Lu Winn, dressed (by Malcolm McLaren) as a pirate

charts sounding and looking only slightly older than she had done when she left the music scene sixteen years earlier. She was fifty-two years old and sexier than all the other teen and twenty-something stars queuing up behind Blondie, desperate to get their song to Number One.

And nobody thought 'That's weird.'

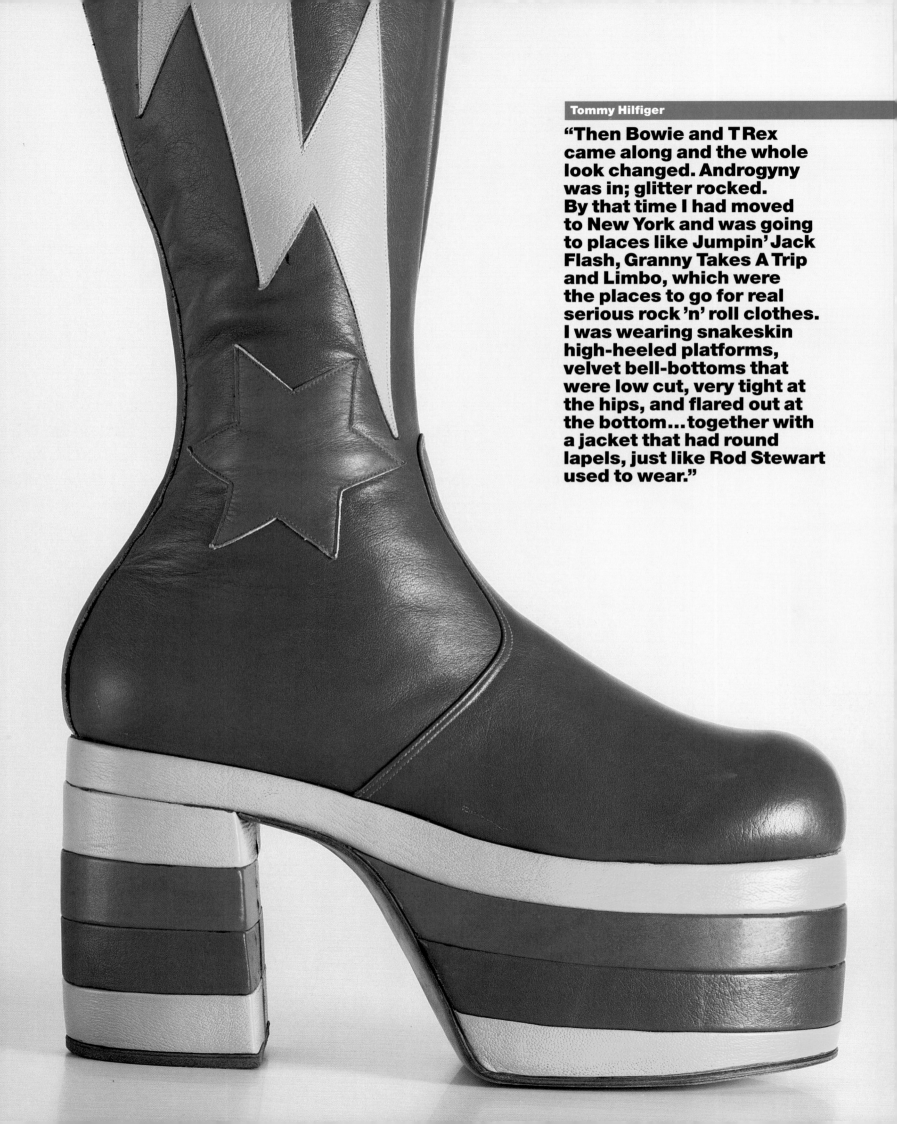

Tommy Hilfiger

"Then Bowie and T Rex came along and the whole look changed. Androgyny was in; glitter rocked. By that time I had moved to New York and was going to places like Jumpin' Jack Flash, Granny Takes A Trip and Limbo, which were the places to go for real serious rock 'n' roll clothes. I was wearing snakeskin high-heeled platforms, velvet bell-bottoms that were low cut, very tight at the hips, and flared out at the bottom...together with a jacket that had round lapels, just like Rod Stewart used to wear."

shoes

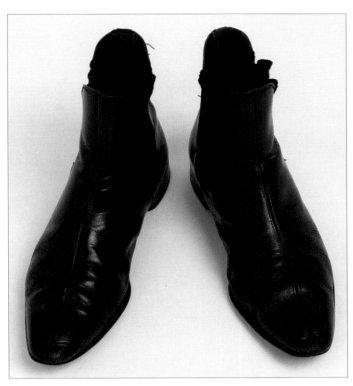

The Beatles' pointy-toed, centre-seamed and, by today's standards, high-heeled versions of the Chelsea boot – known the world over as the Beatle Boot

Tony Calder

"Brian Epstein found these suede boots in a dance shoe shop called Anello And Davide in Mayfair and they were beautifully made, very soft. Because they were dance shoes, of course, they had no soles to speak of, so he had some made with a proper sole and heel and they became known as the Beatle boot. After that Brian Jones used to get all his shoes from there, too."

Jerry Lee Lewis's white shoes stated his rocker credentials at a time when dress was conservative

Few rock stars have made a particular style of shoe their own. Most have simply followed fashion: in the Fifties, Jerry Lee Lewis and Buddy Holly wore points, Gene Vincent, wannabe-rocker-cum-rebel, wore *Wild Ones* biker boots; in the Sixties, The Beach Boys wore sneakers, Donovan hippy sandals; the Seventies saw The Sex Pistols in punky winkle pickers; with the Eighties seeing everything from the Casual movement's Madchester Reeboks to hip-hop Adidas (Run DMC even wrote a homage to the brand, 'My Adidas', while Ice-T name-checked the Chuck Taylor Converse All Star, the style that Mick Jagger, ever remembered in his Eighties aerobics-teacher garb, also chose to marry Bianca in) and little Prince's raised heels. That rock followed fashion was especially true in the Nineties. For a teen band or artist to be seen out of flash if anonymous shoes

1970s rockers were characterised by their new-found height as well as their excessive glamour – Gary Glitter's silver boots were stratospheric

Facing page: Elton John's penchant for wild glasses was perhaps topped only by the colourful stacks of his 1970s footwear.

by the likes of Prada or Patrick Cox or a pair of Nike trainers was rare. The safety of their fashion choices was perhaps reflective of the safety of their product: homogenised, filtered, risqué in a calculated, sales-oriented manner.

But there have, of course, been exceptional predecessors. Elvis, for instance, may forever be associated with blue suede shoes, but this is more to do with the (Carl Perkins-penned) song of the same name, rather than a fashion choice. He rarely appeared in them, although he did most notably with a baby blue shirt with bow-tie and tails on *The Steve Allen Show* for a rendition of 'I Want You, I Need You, I Love You' and 'Hound Dog' (not even the appropriate song). As Elvis pointed out on the show, he had 'on something tonight that's not quite correct for evening wear'. Elvis was more likely to be found in a pair of plain black penny loafers – just like the pair his boyhood singing hero Dean Martin used to wear when he was working the craps table at his local Mafia-run gambling den, slipping silver dollars off the table into the side of his Bass Weejuns.

That other great triumph of rock 'n' roll marketing, The Beatles, had pointy-toed, centre-seamed and, by today's standards, high-heeled versions of the Chelsea boot known the world over as the Beatle Boot. As with all things Beatle, the boot was the brainchild of their manager Brian Epstein. He had previously stumbled upon ballet-shoe makers Anello And Davide in London's Mayfair and been greatly taken with a fine suede boot. The Anello And Davide original, however, had a single rubber composite sole with no heel, and was more like a sixteenth century courtier's boot than that of a swinging Sixties pop star. Once Lennon and McCartney had had their heels felt by the expert cobblers at A&D, they could wear nothing but hand-made shoes. Whose idea it was to put the higher heel on is uncertain, but it generated endless replicas – and a taller public. Even Bob Dylan wore a

pair, although his got a little more dilapidated than those of The Beatles – their manager Brian Epstein would never have allowed it. The boots were another step in making the band seem more of a piece. Even pre-boots and Beatle suits, the group had all worn mock-croc winkle-pinkers (a nod perhaps to their key influences, Chuck Berry and Little Richard), though were prepared to let Pete Best play in non-crocodile versions. The Monkees tried the same approach with suede boots but, like Mike Nesmith's hat, they never caught on.

However, the desert boots worn by The Beatles' only real competition, The Rolling Stones, did. Although off stage they also adored the Anello And Davide boots (Brian Jones being the first to appreciate their elegance), for the cameras they wore Clarks' boots partly to counter the fab four's tidiness. As one Clarks ad at the time put it: 'When new, Clarks' original desert boots are unnecessarily handsome. But with proper loving neglect you can make them look like this in three or four years.' 'Like this' proved to be creased, grubby, broken in: just like the early Rolling Stones.

The style was an odd one to catch the rock world's imagination. Desert boots were modelled on those worn by the British Army officers in the Second World War's North African Desert campaign, and so were symbolic of everything the Stones were against: the upper class, the establishment, the military. The Stones were not alone. Before The Who made the AMC bowling shoe the essential Mod look of the Sixties, one revived in the Nineties by nouveau-mod bands such as Ocean Colour Scene (which made a pair the centre-piece for a single cover), the desert boot did have a moment of Mod approval. But they were eventually seen as being too suburban, safe and class-associated (the wrong class) to go the distance. Such considerations meant little in the Nineties, however, when the likes of Pulp's Jarvis Cocker, Paul Weller and Oasis' Gallagher brothers – all artists with one eye on the past, all with leanings towards a down-to-earth, with-the-people image – took up the style again. But then Liam Gallagher also wore Hush Puppies, traditionally classic pipe and slippers territory.

Almost twenty years prior to the inexorable rise of Manchester's second favourite sons, shoes were already a big deal to rock stars. On the cover of his *Goodbye Yellow Brick Road* album, Elton John is about to step through a magical doorway into a

The Skinhead movement – characterised in dress by green MA1 flight jackets, denim jackets, Harringtons, gingham shirts, jeans with tight turn-ups, braces (the braces were often abandoned when tighter-fitting Levi's were adopted) and leather boots (often Dr Marten's, worn with colour-coded laces) – had close musical associations, from ska bands to the likes of Madness and Bad Manners in the 1980s

rainbow-dipped Land of Oz. That's if he makes it. He's wearing a pair of towering yellow platforms, and has one foot raised to the doorway. The boot, not the vista or even Elton's glasses, are the star of the cover. A favourite showman trick of his was to stand and dance on his Steinway in his platforms. The point was not climbing onto the piano – that had been done by just about every rocking piano-player around – but getting on it in these 'EJ' monogrammed, silver, red and white leather stacks. That deserved applause. And if it is true that you can tell a man by his shoes, what can you say about Elton's love of platforms – that he has a troubled soul? Or that he's just conscious of his height?

In the 1975 movie *Tommy,* based on the 1969 album by The Who, Elton John was the Pinball Wizard. He wore a massive pair of Dr Marten boots, almost as big as him. The pair eventually returned to Dr Marten's when the managing director bought them at a sale of rock memorabilia at Sotheby's – in the meantime the boots had helped make Dr Marten's a cult item. Utilitarian, basic, comfortable, DMs could not be further away from Elton's usual footwear.

Elton John as the Pinball Wizard in Tommy, *wearing giant Dr Marten lace-up boots*

But this was the Seventies. Everybody was wearing bad parodies of Forties style. Couture shoemaker Vivier stacked a sandal in 1967 and by the end of the decade the look had reached London. And Elton. Barbara Hulanicki's Biba store offered a five-inch heel and sold 75,000 pairs. The look took off, almost literally, with *The Sunday Times* reporting in 1971 on 'monster boots with vast club-like wedges, weighty legacies from the hideous Victoriana of Lancashire mills.' Sold – the rest of the decade saw every glam-rock group in both the UK and US, from Kiss to Alice Cooper and the New York Dolls, from Sweet to Slade to Marc Bolan, Gary Glitter and Alvin Stardust, up there on platforms. The height elevated their egos to new heights, their choice of footwear shaping the nation's. They were rock stars at a time when rock stars were supposed to wear silly clothes. The public just looked on, and up, in admiration.

Only a handful, or perhaps a footful, of other rockers have come as close to Elton as being identified with a shoe of their own.

1970s British glam rock was nothing if not excessive, characterised by a sexually-ambiguous style that crossed over from American funk and would lead to disco. Marc Bolan became a leading exponent, having moved on from Mod to hippie and then to glam. But while the likes of The Sweet blockbusted both musically and in footwear terms, Bolan chose to wear ballet pumps to emphasise his already slight frame

That rock stars could be used to sell fashion items was not lost to footwear brand leaders Kickers

ROGER DALTREY
WEARS
KicKers

331 Kings Road, Chelsea, London S.W.
66 South Molton Street, London W.1.
and at Top Shop, Oxford Circus, W.1.
Telephone: 01-351 1433

Facing page: Prefiguring 1970s knee-high boots, as popularised by Abba, Lulu covers her legs with her footwear where her outfit has failed

The Who's Pete
Townshend in his
Dr Marten's

Shoes for most seem to have been an after-thought, not a garment considered important in image-building or self-expression, more simply a means of getting from limo to dressing-room to stage to bar in some degree of comfort.

It would be the late Seventies/early Eighties before a single shoe brand captured the rock imagination again. And that, once again, was the Dr Marten boot. Worn initially by The Who's Pete Townshend (enabling him to bounce around on stage) and then, more famously, by Madness, the DM was a sensible counter to the gaudy glam years that had preceded it – from the impractical knee-high boots of Abba through the flash snakeskin cowboy boots of Gram Parsons – the DM was very un-rock 'n' roll: tough, sensible, mother's choice, with a sole as resistant to oil, fat and acid as most rock stars are weak to white powder and willing groupies, the DM was the perfect shoe for Madness, about as down-to-earth a pop outfit as possible. Worn with all-done-up pale suit, bowler, leather driving gloves and Northampton-made DMs, front-man Suggs looked every inch the parody of the Englishness and the Gentleman spirit that the lyrics frequently considered. The shoes, with their yellow welt stitching, even had grooves running around the side of the two-tone sole, like a vinyl record. With their skinhead roots, the DM shoe was also the obvious choice for the band; DM 1460 eight-eyelet boots were part of the classic skinhead uniform, and the band originally sported the full Monty of boots, crop and MA1 flight jacket.

It wasn't long before the DM became established as the footwear of the UK's alternative rock scene, an emblem of both Goth and punk. But while Ocean Colour Scene used the bowling shoe to signify their affiliation to Mod, the bowling shoe did not instantly translate back to the band. The DM says Madness. Few shoes have this resonance. There is only one other band that has been so closely associated with a particular style that the two have become interchangeable, that sales of the shoe have rocketed in line with sales of their records, that, Beatle-like, they have been able to market the shoe as a quintessential band product. The style echoes Elton John's one-time preference but

Emma Bunton,
aka Baby Spice of
the Spice Girls, in
the highest
footwear since
Glam. In Britain
The Spice Girls
kick-started a
craze in platform
trainers, led by the
Buffalo brand

The Clash in
Northern Ireland
in 1977

Graham McPherson, aka Suggs, suedehead frontman of Madness and Dr Marten fan

"Photography was a hugely important element of *The Face* at the beginning, the most important element. It was a photo book with words, I was trying to produce a version of *Time* or *Life* that held a mirror up to pop culture, what it wore, where it went, what it listened to. That iconic imagery I'd used at the *NME*, I wanted to run like a thread through *The Face*, unsullied by the clutter of advertising. Everything in the first few issues was a photographic essay about style and music – whether it was Madness in New York shot by Jill Furmanovsky, Dexy's Midnight Runners by Mike Laye, or a series of early rockabilly photos of the young Elvis Presley. There was no question as far as I was concerned that this was as much a fashion magazine as it was a music magazine, though of course it was done by stealth. It only came into the open when the New Romantics started dressing up. Later, when *The Face* began to run more overt fashion pages and tag them 'Style', the early models were musicians, people like Suggs, John Cooper Clarke and Heaven 17 shot by Sheila Rock."

Nick Logan, founder of *The Face*

Facing page:
Sandie Shaw had
the simple, hippie
solution to every
rocker's footwear
dilemma –
go barefoot

DEXTER

DEXTER SHOE COMPANY
31 ST. JAMES AVE.
BOSTON, MASS. 02116

*The 1970s taste
in lifted and
clownish footwear
wasn't lost on the
smarter brands,
who capitalised
on an association
with the more
outrageous
glam rockers,
'Blockbuster' here
also referring to
The Sweet song*

BLOCKBUSTER

with a Nineties athletic twist: the platform trainer, as worn by the Spice Girls, notably by their younger fans' favourites Baby Spice Emma Bunton and ex-Spicer Ginger Geri Halliwell. Making them superhumanly tall was the ideal way to make two of the group's more average looking members stand out. And fall over. Such was the impact of these ugly shoes, part Nike, part orthopaedic, that when Bunton took a fall in them, twisting her ankle, it made front-page national news. The style was even considered dangerous and banned from some schools. It should have been banned everywhere.

Footwear does say much about the wearer but it is hard to get it right. Perhaps that is why there is such considerable indifference to footwear among rock and pop people. It's best ignored. Sandie Shaw had the right idea thirty-five years before the Spice Girls. She didn't wear any shoes at all.

*Robbie Williams,
shod in line with
the 1990's
sneaker boom and
in the dressed
down styling of
teen-orientated
groups of the time
(among them All
Saints), here
wearing Merrell
cross-trainers*

*Blue Suede Shoes
– the most famous
footwear in rock*

There was more rebellion in Elvis' hair than in any hip-wiggle or snarl. These 'five inches of hot-buttered yak wool', as one *Time* magazine commentator put it, marked a new era – in music, in fashion – and also marked a movement toward excess after post-war austerity. Show business had arrived after the war wearing its hair longer, looser. Elvis had been a fan of Dean Martin since he could watch a movie and walk the walk. Dino's hair was greased and slightly quiffed, worn, unusually and unacceptably long for the late Forties, it had the appearance of being jet black. Elvis took Dino's style and emphasised it tenfold. He swept it back over his ears into a duck's ass, added side-burns and allowed the piled high hair to tumble down over his forehead in a parody of Sinatra's former bobby-soxing kiss-curls. (Ten years later, with Elvis relegated to unthreatening mediocre film fodder, Dino's former sparring partner Jerry Lewis would emulate Elvis emulating Dino in *The Nutty Professor* for his take on a dangerous lounge singer; Lewis' hair slicked even higher and oilier).

As with everything else he did, Elvis's hair made a statement. Although Sinatra, Dino and jazz trumpeter Gerry Mulligan had inspired white styles before Presley, they did not inspire imitators. Or rebellion – their styles were takes on the norm. Presley's made hair the defining moment of birth for rock fashion. Scenes of his head being shaved for army service in 1958 – Presley sitting in the barber's chair, his expression a confusion of fear and a bemused smile, the cameras clicking as the number four razor passed especially slowly through the locks – was like watching Samson being shorn of his strength. For many it was the end of rock 'n' roll, the birth of a new era in which sexuality wore tidy suits and pudding-bowl cuts.

That hair should be so important to rock fashion was due to its accessibility. In the beginning, rocks stars *were* stars: Elvis' first tours, of hayrides, fairgrounds and schools in the Deep South, had

Dean Martin, Dino, Rat Packer and super-slick, both in attitude and hair

The hair-cut that defined a generation – buttered yak wool, greased and creased

"Elvis Presley singing 'Baby I Don't Care' poolside in *Jailhouse Rock*, hair as immaculate as Sean Penn in *Dead Man Walking* minus, natch, the bumfluff. The tight-ribbed cable knit, shirt, collared sweater, the mohair tonic-ish loose black trews and the black and white immaculate weight shoes personified cool by the pool. All cash, all dash. Health is wealth. An immaculate Presley moment."

Andrew Loog Oldham, manager of The Rolling Stones

Facing page:
The King is dead.
Long live the King.
The haircut that began the decline of Presley's career

Piled high, Elvis' haircut allowed his rampant sexuality to be on show even while the 1950's TV cameras refused to film him below the waist

*A young, pre-militant
Malcolm X, hair
straightened like a
white man's and
heading towards a
conk. Malcolm's
increasing black
awareness was
echoed in his later
wearing his hair
curled and cropped*

Following pages:
Clockwise from top
left: Ike Turner, with
the conk; Bill Haley,
originator of the
cow-lick; Little
Richard, with
smoothed-out
super-conk; and
Cliff Richard,
England's own Elvis.
Full page: Esquerita,
style role model to
Little Richard

Little Miss Dynamite, Brenda Lee with de rigeur high hair

Connie Francis in twin set, pearls and Peter Pan-like bouffant

physically positioned him high up, above the heads of the crowds, so that the spectators at the front were given a full vantage view of the shaking, quaking pelvis – Elvis had to be untouchable, back-lit and burning brightly and often briefly. Elvis decreed that rock stars dressed differently, that they were different. Their clothes had to be beyond imitation. Only the hair could be copied with any degree of success – both by the fans and other groups, first in homage and then in a playful referencing which echoed through the subsequent decades and saw the pomaded pompadour begin in rebellion and end up on super-smoothy Bryan Ferry. When Elvis combed his hair, women would scream. Some, according to a *Life* magazine story in 1957, even copied his hairstyle. Teds and bikers, ever the closest of street fashions, copied him, the former burnt-corking in sideburns if necessary, pulling the wings of their DAs round into the elephant trunk like Jimmy Clanton's – a look later emphasised to the point of buffoonery in a late Seventies rockabilly movement.

The most visible female role models in rock and roll was Jayne Mansfield, the star of The Girl Can't Help It. So enduring was her image that Madonna would, over thirty years later, take inspiration from her looks

But while black America pushed on with hair history – Esquerita, Little Richard, Ike Turner all wearing 'dos of stratospheric height, processed, whipped up and blow-dried into a conk, a style that later became a mark of the black man's subjugation to the white – Britain in the early Sixties was producing styles you could take home to mother. Country and western music had inspired women to wear the pony-tail, a style as inoffensive as the songs of exponent Brenda Lee, or styles short but high, like Alma Cogan and Connie Francis. But it was the bouffant, Dusty Springfield's inverted Walnut Whip confection of lacquered hair, or the descriptively-named beehive, that was the first sign that the Sixties would be a decade in which the style of rock 'n' roll would become truly fixed, when the ironic uniformity of rock star style became ingrained in the collective consciousness of the world. From the last days of the Sixties the idea of the quiff, long fringes, beehives and pageboy cuts would instantly conjure up the sound of whoever wore it that way. After Diana Ross, The Beatles and Jim Morrison, hair was safe again. The Supremes went as far as doing away with all Presley-ish preening

Jim Morrison, hair heavy and long for the latter-day Byronic poet

"Teds and Pop made the working class the arbiters of style."

Nik Cohn, cultural critic

Twenty five years after Teddy Boys were first spotted in the aisles of cinemas across Britain, a revival of the style supported a network of specialist record shops, invented a rockabilly sub-genre and saw quiffs and Brothel Creeper shoes back on the sticky carpets of flea pits across the nation

Diana Ross And The Supremes, looking supreme in a bubble-permed Afro

for ready-made wigs of towering styles: Morrison made uncombed tumbling pre-Raphaelite curls the foundation stone for wannabe doomed rock poets. Both styles were easy to achieve. By the Seventies the idea of working on your hair was, like the world at large, outdated. The idea of working at all was, by then of course, not very rock 'n' roll at all.

As with almost everything else in the history of rock 'n' roll, The Beatles provided the second seismic shock to civilised society's system. The cover of *With The Beatles* said it all: four hovering faces, their bodies fading into the black, their fringes straighter than sheet music staves. It was the manager Brian Epstein – the first manager to realise that pop groups would have to be marketed as a complete image-centric package – who took The Beatles away from their own efforts at Elvis slick-ups and gave them an originality that made them nearer to their fans than Elvis had been, enforcing a uniformity of look which was skilfully manipulated to emphasise the individuality of their personalities. Everything about the outward appearance of The Beatles matched, from their overgrown pudding-bowl cuts, to their (Pierre Cardin-inspired) collarless jacket suits, Chelsea boots, shirts and ties. The mop top had first been modelled by deceased former art student Beatle Stuart Sutcliffe, as styled by his German girlfriend Astrid Kirchherr, and based on Jean Marais' hairstyle as Oedipus in Cocteau's 1959 *Le Testament d'Orphée*.

Away with the Elvis slicks, in with the mummy's boy mop tops for The Beatles – though the style was still particularly long for the early 1960s

Epstein's choice of style for the Fab Four was dry – no Grease Grease Me – yet it retained a rebellious edge. For the time, it was long hair, and caused U.S. President Lyndon Johnson to famously ask The Beatles to "go get a haircut". It was, of course, copied all over the planet and in America inspired the only authentic Beatle wig ('Wow! The Beatles are here!', hollered the packaging). Far from being the peak of insurrection, the mop top became cute and wholesome, perched like a schoolboy

The Beatles were the first British act to be aggressively marketed to middle America using spin-off merchandising. Witness this ad for a Beatle Wig. Or is it George?

cap over All-American chipmunk grins. Prophetically, one-time Beatles drummer Pete Best always refused to adopt the hair-cut. He was later sacked by the rest of the band.

As legend has it, The Rolling Stones made rock 'n' roll dangerous and sexy again in the mid-Sixties. The Stones preached rebellion wearing a roughed-up, ruffled, grown-out mop top – at best it was an approximation of the Regency style that looked, ideally, like they'd

Stuart Sutcliffe, the fifth Beatle and the man who, via his girlfriend, shaped the mop top, shown sporting a fine back-combed quiff

Page-boy cuts for The Kinks – a decadent style that suited their dandy dressing perfectly

"Hair was a kind of religion with The Kinks and The Pretty Things. Growing one's hair was also an overwhelmingly middle-class style of revolt."

Nik Cohn

just got out of bed. Their music might have been second-rate R&B speeded up to disguise the lack of musical ability on show, but their hair saved their early bacon. It was the only element of doubt in an otherwise tamely-dressed group who appeared on *Ready Steady Go!* in neat slacks and chunky sweaters. With this cut, they looked like yobs and upset fathers across the land. '[Other bands] were all crew-cut, that was the style,' noted Bill Wyman of the group's first appearances in the U.S. '[So there were] people shouting, 'Are you girls?', 'Are you The Beatles?', saying sarcastic things like, 'You could see the fleas jumping off their heads' and 'They smelled'.'

Neat cuts for All American Boys The Beach Boys

After the Stones invaded America, hair once more became an anti-establishment statement. The wise guys got it. 'You know these singing groups today, you're under the impression they have long hair,' said Dino on the *Ed Sullivan Show*. 'Not true at all. It's an optical illusion: they all have low foreheads and high eyebrows.' For any

The Rolling Stones' Keith Richards with carefree hair – and prefiguring the shag of Rod Stewart

young rock group, it was a call to arms. The Kinks and any other progressive group with art house pretensions took up the look or a derivative of it. Only

The Rolling Stones' Mick Jagger, all lip and long hair

Facing page: Brian Jones, a wild man with wild looks, the hair seeming to merge seamlessly with the sideburns

hair **172**

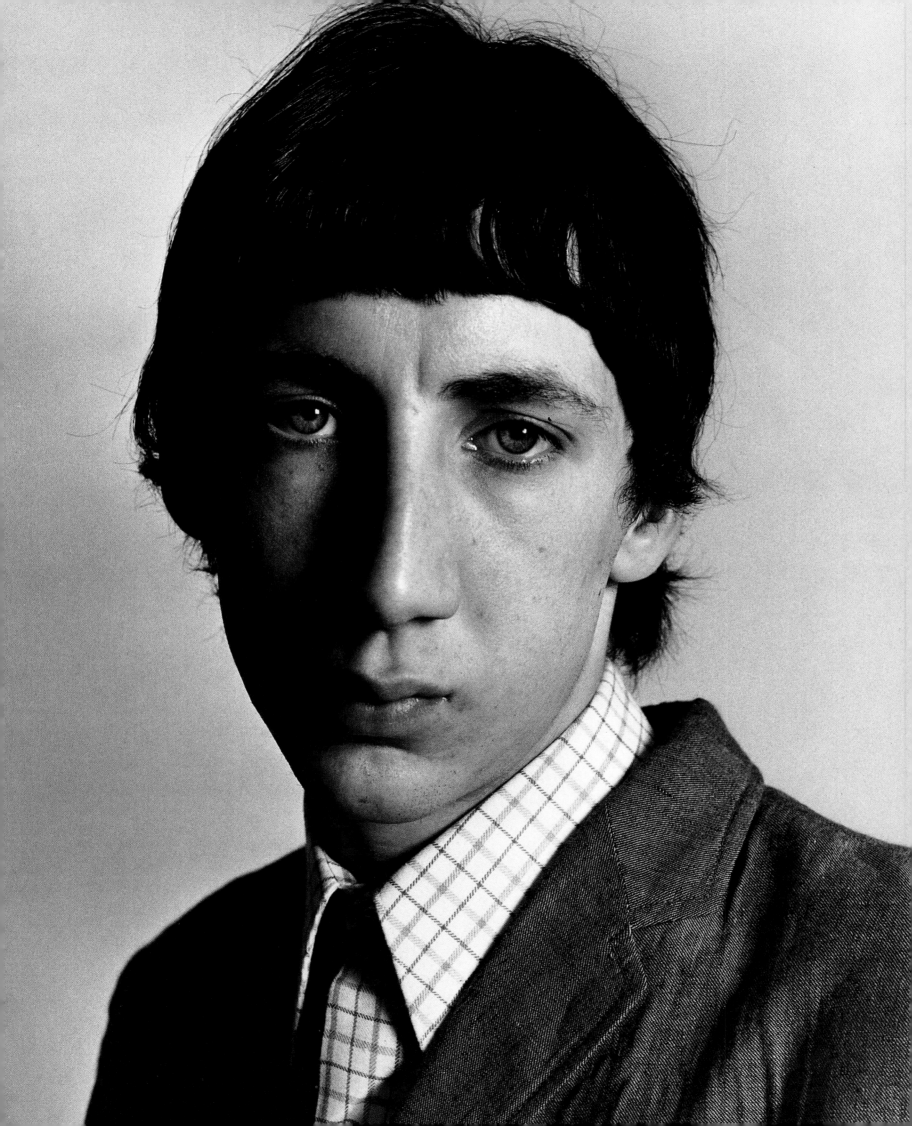

The Byrds in pudding-bowl cuts with fringes, post-Beatles almost hippy

Rod 'The Mod' Stewart, centre, with a grown-out version of his previous Mod cut, alongside (L-R) Jeff Beck, Mickey Waller and Ronnie Wood

the Americans stayed true to short and neat: witness the crew or basin cuts of the Beach Boys, just like mama would have cut it.

From the late Sixties on, however, long hair was de rigeur for any rock act. The early Seventies was the first period in which rock stars sought not to be elevated above the crowd, but to be part of the people's movement, in which the (love) generation encompassed famous and anonymous, filthy rich and just filthy alike. Hair was an expression of a new attitude, a free-for-all of styles not seen again until the Nineties. But most of these styles had bohemian, free-livin', spiritual overtones. Crosby Stills And Nash sang 'Almost Cut My Hair'. Jim Morrison's shag-pile curls made him both Byronic and sex machine, rock monsters Ted Nugent and Robert Plant expressed base, guttural, Neanderthal leanings with monolithic manes of unkempt abandon. Even former short and sharp Mod stylists such as The Who's Roger Daltrey, Marc Bolan and Rod Stewart had allowed their ordered hairlines to grow out. By the beginning of the age of Aquarius, girlie long-hair was all man.

But such artless cuts couldn't last. There was to be a reaction against a style made lazy with love and mellowing drugs. Even if the rock mantra was born to be wild, mid-Seventies preening, look-at-me glam was more born to be styled. Fashion became a culture of mass production and mass consumption, something everybody did. In the UK art colleges started producing pop groups as interested in the cut of their clothes and hair as cutting the next record. David Bowie, for one, moved through influential

Classic Rod Stewart style, hair down to his shoulders but short on top

Rock excess brought long, long hair everywhere – head, face, chest, lapels... chief exponents Led Zeppelin

Facing page: Pete Townshend of The Who with his Mod-inspired straight fringe

haircuts as often as he changed musical style. From a very feminine mess of blonde waves on the cover of *The Man Who Sold The World*, through the peroxide straw-blonde crop of *Ziggy Stardust* to the dandelion puff-ball of *Pin-Ups* and the red-head new-bouffant, slicked at the sides, long at the back, of *Aladdin Sane* and *Diamond Dogs*, Bowie moved haircuts along at a breakneck speed until the day he stopped inventing, went to Canvey Island (lair of the UK's home-grown soulboy scene which would later evolve into the Casuals of the Eighties) and adopted the blue-eyed soulboy look of long, flicked wedge fringe of *Young Americans*. Bowie's album covers were a manual of the decade's androgynous hair style, a shock tactic of artificial colour, quiff and blow-drying influencing the peroxide vamp of Annie Lennox and copied well into the Eighties by the likes of Goth Madame Siouxsie Sioux and synthpop exponents on both sides of the Atlantic. It was a high concept hair-cut, the kind only the rock and pop fraternity could get away with, one as archly considered as the Sex Pistol spikes. Roxy Music's Bryan Ferry and Rod Stewart also produced seminal haircuts. Ferry moved from a wet-look take on the Fifties elephant trunk to the mannequin polyester wig look later espoused by John Travolta as the hair-aware Tony Manero in 1977's *Saturday Night Fever*.

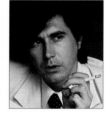

Mannequin-made man Bryan Ferry, naturally not a hair out of place

Ferry's was a new look for pop people, a much copied (at least there were many attempts) step away from the rough and ready towards a more sophisticated lounge singer look. Even Stewart – already long regarded as the definitive lad – opted for a genderless shag style that was as much part of the Seventies as flares and wide collars. The hair was as out of control as Stewart liked to think he was: heavy at the sides and back, wild and tufty on top. Cross-bred, the styles of Bowie, Ferry and Stewart show a distinct shift to the big hair styles of the end of the decade and the beginnings of the Eighties.

Punks appropriated the Teddy Boy quiff, made it spiky and also upset a lot of old Teds

One of the distinctive and thankfully rarely copied hairstyles of the 1980s, courtesy of A Flock Of Seagulls

Billy Idol, below, with trademark sneer and bleached blonde spikes

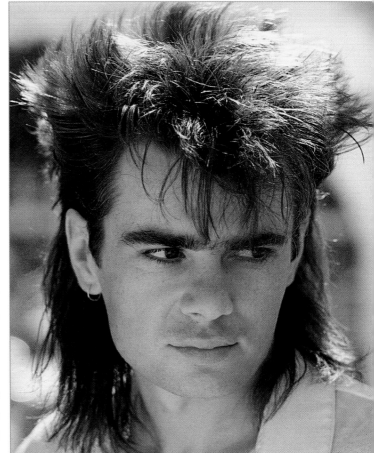

Nik Kershaw in the popular 1980s cut – the mullet, here worn gelled

Punk had championed the comic assassination of the original Elvis quiff: exaggerated to the point of Tex Avery ludicrousness with Vaseline and KY Jelly, dyed in shades of middle-aged spinsterdom, Rotten, Vicious and Idol spat their Elvis hair into shocking shapes that went too far and soon became a parody of itself – these days the best punk spiked quiff is to be found atop the two-dimensional heads of Bart and Lisa Simpson. But at least the classic Punk quiff wasn't easy or lazy. It took time to make it work. Ironically, unlike the music, punk's hair was a labour intensive activity. Paradoxically, Rotten, Strummer, Vicious, Sioux and Co reintroduced the fashion for rock stars to dress up to look different from their fans. It was an idea seized upon by a new generation of rock stars who apparently enjoyed dressing up a lot more than making new or original music.

The Eighties became the melting pot for fashion and hairstyles alike. The glitter, glitz, fright-night stage make-up and self-re-invention of the Seventies segued into something altogether more random and experimental to the point of bad taste. The decade began with the music industry in crisis, with sales at an all-time low and the conglomerates who owned the business desperate to find new ways of making a buck. The mainstream was splitting. Rock music was growing up and having children who wanted something else, something new to get excited about. Media pundits predicted that computers, games and all that went with it would mean the end of the pop music business. It had to diversify and the sub-genre was born. With each new section in the record stores came a stark look designed to generate both difference and publicity and the beginnings of the post-modern haircut: Sigue Sigue Sputnik, short-lived hi-tech power popsters, opted for multi-coloured mohicans that nodded to punk, while Duran Duran and Wham! went Seventies Bee Gee highlighted bouffant, Eurythmics' Annie Lennox tried a cropped Ziggy, Cyndi Lauper a grown-out one, Morrissey took on the Fifties with a nouveau quiff, Prince with a processed Latino conk and Nik Kershaw hacked at

The Eurythmics, Annie Lennox with Dave Stewart – the tidy and the electrified

Pin-up punk. The Clash's Paul Simonon with layered, spiky crop

Morrissey, 1950s-inspired (and much imitated by student fans) in both hair and dress

Neo-rockabillies The Stray Cats, with a nod to the 1950s via updated and impressive elephant trunks

179 suits

Mick Hucknall, with add-on dreadlocks

Facing page: *low maintenance hair meant twisting it into clumps and never washing it. It cost you friends*

Rod Stewart's shag to create the cut (a mullet) worn by footballers and the Casual movement for much of the decade.

The dreadlock came out of Jamaica into the mainstream, helped along by the punks. Where it had once been the look of true religion, worn only by Rastas, in the early Eighties a bunch of Notting Hill Trustafarians (boys and girls living on a trust fund, playing Big Leggy in ripped trews and woolly hats) put Dread extensions in their hair and perfectly, un-ironically echoed the prophetic words of Joe Strummer in 'White Man (In Hammersmith Palais)': 'You think it's funny, turning rebellion into money.' Hayzee Fantayzee, Green of Scritti Politti (although his were at least real) and later Mick Hucknall all favoured the dread look.

Meanwhile, Goths, among them The Cure's Robert Smith, self-cut, back-combed and black-dyed into a gravity-defying puff-ball without frontiers (when Smith cut it all off in 1986 the reaction of the MTV generation was almost comparable to that generated by Elvis's army cut), and a new era in solo 'girlfriend' acts, among them Tiffany from the US and the UK-adopted Australian Kylie Minogue, captured the market for wet perms. The queen of trash couture, Madonna, expressed herself with hair recently caught in a hurricane, an abandoned but much mimicked style. It was the best of times, it was the worst of times for fashion. Anything went.

New Romanticism required big hair, colour, highlights, lacquered flicks. Spandau Ballet hit the mark

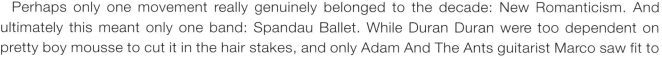

Perhaps only one movement really genuinely belonged to the decade: New Romanticism. And ultimately this meant only one band: Spandau Ballet. While Duran Duran were too dependent on pretty boy mousse to cut it in the hair stakes, and only Adam And The Ants guitarist Marco saw fit to

Back-combed and hair-sprayed, the Goth hair of Robert Smith of The Cure

Theatrically coiffed Romantics Duran Duran

Don't You Want Me, Baby? Phil Oakey of Human League, with his distinctive peek-a-boo bang

go NR as a pirate, the Ballet boys wore a side-parted wedge with an over-long fringe that drooped dramatically (and obstructively) over an eye. The look had originally been worn to devastating effect in Forties Hollywood by Veronica Lake and christened the 'peek-a-boo bang'. The 'bang' was taken to an extreme conclusion by Phil Oakey of the Human League and worn by every Eighties teen worth his eclectic wardrobe.

The Eighties – a decadent decade is retrospect – was also to be the last era of rock hairdos to remember. By the end of the decade the rock community had turned to embrace its public rather than to differentiate itself from it. These one-time quifftastic super-beings decided that it was best to look ordinary. There have been notable cuts on individuals – George Michael's sweep-forward Brutus crop, the distinctive ginger dreads of Mick Hucknall, even the Natalie, a scruffy page-boyish look so popular it could be referred to by its first name only, though named after popstress Natalie Imbruglia.

But most Nineties cuts saw rockers grow old: they began to follow hair fashion rather than define it. Only two rock-inspired trends emerged distinct from the pre-millennial decade, and they couldn't be

The hair that launched a thousand copies during the late 1990s – the Natalie, named after post-soap pop songstress Natalie Imbruglia

The white trash look inspired by Madonna and widely borrowed – here by Bananarama – straggly, badly dyed and harshly back-combed

Facing page: *Bombshell Deborah Harry of Blondie, showing off Jean Harlow-inspired platinum tresses*

Jon Bon Jovi during the mid-1980s – big rock hair for a big rock sound

Kurt Cobain of Nirvana, the king of grunge, symbolised its lack of interest in hair-care

more different. On the one hand there was Nirvana and Kurt Cobain's grunge, the Seventies love god meets rock animal mess of unwashed tresses – copied only by the lonely and a style eventually cut short by Cobain in a particularly permanent manner. And on the other hand, the scalped – distinctive on women such as the aptly-named Skin of Skunk Anansie, shaved and then slightly grown-out by Sinead O'Connor and adopted by the likes of R.E.M's Michael Stipe, more for personal than fashion reasons. There wasn't much else between them.

By the end of the Nineties, rock 'n' roll seemed to have run out of steam in all departments. It was sartorially challenged to the point of being ruled by fashion's hippest designers – 'cutting-edge' rock stars appear as models either on or at the front row of shows by new, happening cloth-cutters where once it was the other way around. Haircuts became nothing more than rock 'n' roll clichés. If you're into metal you wore it long and

Grace Jones with short hair. At various times, Jones also wore her own take on the conk and a severe but scientifically-precise flat-top

The well-clipped Sinead O'Connor, a harsh cut that highlighted her natural beauty

Michael Stipe of REM, wisely dispensing with hair when he began to lose it, replacing it with odd variations in facial hair

Facing page: The aptly-named skinhead movement attracted musical followers who passed on the tattoo

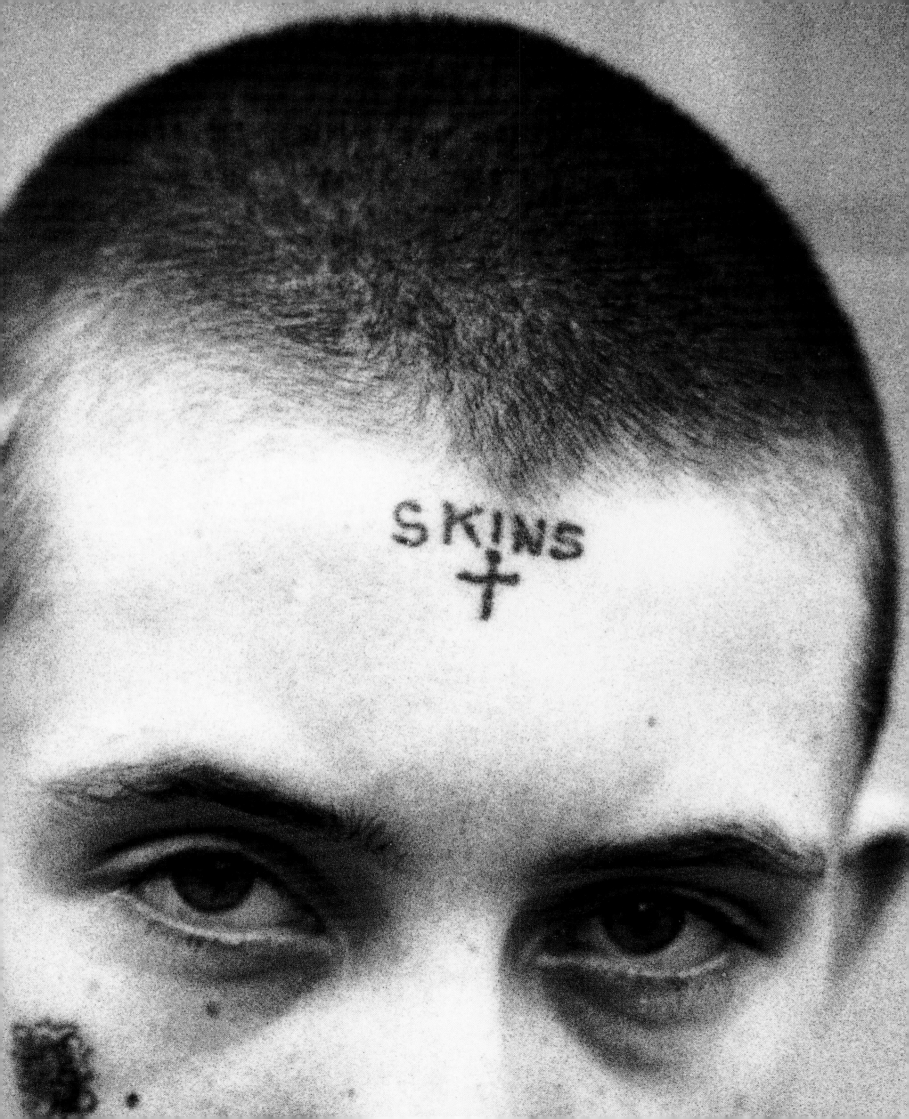

unwashed. Ditto for grunge. If you were into hip-hop it was perhaps worn razor cut with maybe a designer logo thrown in. Soul still meant the wedge; Country still meant the higher the hair, the closer to God; Psychedelics all owned the same Roger McGuinn-inspired pudding bowl; while Elvis impersonators the world over still worked their hair up and over, dyed it jet black and sported sideburns to park Cadillacs in.

Even original rock talents had hair problems. As Björk, who invented the Mickey Mouse-style pig-tail look, said: 'Before you get famous, you've got hair, right, and it grows a bit. So it grew a bit. People come up to me now and say, "You've got a new image!" 'Cause of hair.'

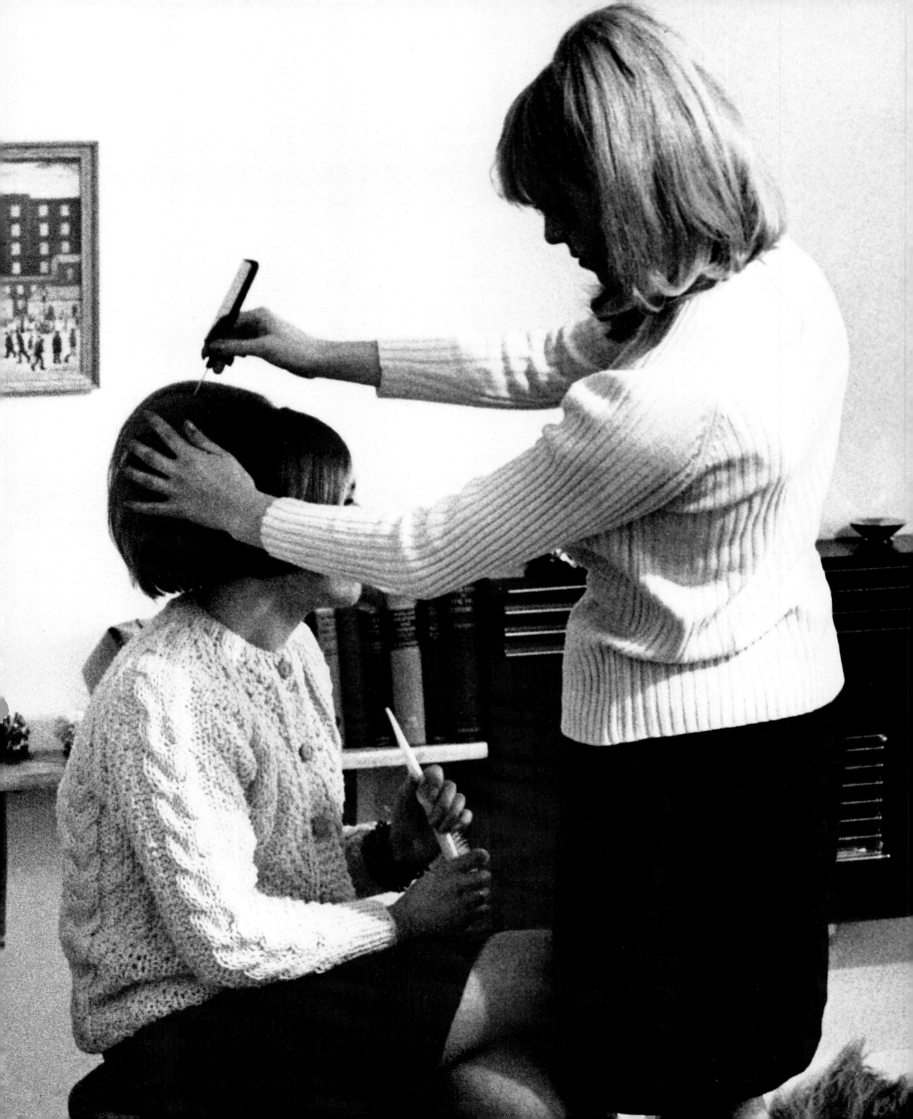

Facing page:
Embryonic Beehive being pomped with obligatory steel comb, circa 1964

The Chairman Of The Board sport their Afros proudly

Stevie Wonder, perhaps best known in hair terms for his rasta beaded dreads, but here with 'parted' close crop

Top Right:
A young Michael Jackson with Afro, before having both his nose and his hair straightened

Slade, in pre-Glam days, mixing up Mod influences, suedehead and pudding-bowl cuts

The Beatles, top of the mops, with coiffured fans

Garbage in, garbage out: Music figures such as Shirley Manson no longer influence fashion designers

"There isn't very much individualism in rock fashion anymore. Most bands just wear baggy trousers and a T-shirt, which is fairly bland. And in a sense that is true of the music. Perhaps music and fashion originality goes hand in hand, but I think it's more that at my age you've seen and heard it all before, so it takes something really new to surprise me. Don't get me wrong – I listen to a lot of current music: I love The Manic Street Preachers, Garbage. But there aren't many bands that have a real influence on fashion now."

Paul Smith

make-up|face

Since the first stage was built, public performance has involved a degree of gender confusion. Shakespeare's plays are full of men dressing as women, women as men, boys as women and girls as boys. Make-up, of course, helps to further blur the sexual identity of a performer. Rock 'n' roll was always about showing off, about sexual, emotional and physical discovery – the things that any teenager is curious about. Both Elvis and Little Richard wore make-up on stage; as did any other performer in front of lights and cameras, even the most determinedly heterosexual. Combined with their flamboyant dress, though, Elvis and Richard Penniman were somehow more threatening. It was as if the combination of their sexually-charged, hip-thrusting, guttural performances challenged the 'normal' conventions of masculinity. That they made girls scream and boys squirm was exactly why they were so successful; both sexes had natural teen anxieties about their sexual preferences. Elvis and Little Richard set the ground rules in rock 'n' roll make-up, determining that if you're going to make an impression in the rock business, you need a big face, a striking one. You need, as Madonna sang in 'Vogue', to be able to give good face.

Since the 1950s, doing so has been more subtle for some than for others, but no less memorable. Midge Ure, once of Ultravox, will forever be remembered for his razor-sharp bespoke sideburns that swept victoriously forward and had been 'borrowed' from Gene Vincent. Kraftwerk are held in the minds eye as looking a bit peaky, with their mannequin or android paleness appropriate to their part

Facing page: Marianne Faithfull's un-made-up au naturel look

Following pages: In rock both men and women wear the make-up – here, Little Richard and Sandie Shaw

"Every girl has a favourite colour. I have 26," says Mary Quant.

in inventing robotic synthesiser music, a look later used by Gary Numan. The members of ZZ Top are remembered for their endless beards. Think of Goldie and, like name, like nature, you think of his gold teeth. Keith Flint of Prodigy is synonymous with kohl-black eyes and ironmongery through his nose. Each has a visual twist that is essential to leaving a mark on a public faced with endless musical choices.

Few, however, inspired imitation in fashion circles, although fans followed in droves. For them, the ultimate identification with their heroes was not just to wear the tour T-shirt or the outfit, but to adopt the face. Teeny-bopper fans copied the glued-on sequins, liberally-applied mascara and painted stars of Sweet or Slade, the glitter of Marc Bolan, but it took a brighter star to make a face resonate with youth culture and maintain artistic credibility.

In 1972, shortly before the release of another album hot on the heels of *Hunky Dory,* David Bowie made ripples in 'normal society' by announcing his bisexuality in an interview with *Melody Maker.* He'd slipped into an elegant, patterned type of combat suit, very tight around the legs, with the shirt unbuttoned to reveal

Bare-faced liar.

a full expanse of white torso, wrote the interviewer. The trousers were turned up at the calves to allow a better

PERFUME IN A SWINGING MOOD GiGi

glimpse of a huge pair of red plastic shoes; and the hair was Vidal Sassoon-ed into such impeccable shape that one held one's breath in case the slight breeze from the open window dared to ruffle it.

It was a wild style, even for then. But the real shock was yet to come. When *The Rise And Fall Of Ziggy Stardust And The Spiders From Mars* was released, a new rock character was created. It took *Aladdin Sane* to add the final touch: a burnt orange zig-zag, lined with blue and streaking over Bowie's face, across his eyes. The invention of such a stage character was a brilliant piece of marketing: the make-up slash was an instant trademark that also created a visual precedent for rock star imagery. This stylised Z was projected as a back-drop at concerts while rumours abounded that it had sinister Nazi SS connotations. Indeed, Bowie's manager Tony DeFries had said that he saw Bowie as a large scale untouchable. 'He doesn't quite belong here,' he said. Ziggy was a fictional, sexually ambiguous (and stereotype-challenging) alien rock superstar and all it took was the make-up.

A pulp novel of the time, *Glam* by Richard Allen, told the tale of how 'Johnny Holland fights to stay the idol of a million fans'. On its cover, Johnny Holland has had markedly less success than Bowie in putting on his stripes and looks more like a child's attempt at face painting. But Bowie's fans had more success in copying the flash. Fans looked startling in their copy-cat outfits. There was no doubting their homage. This was adolescent make-believe of the first order. DeFries clearly had a sensation on his hands. Plans for Ziggy dolls were put in place, for Ziggy jump suits and boots, none of which came to fruition (even without this, Bowie was to later say that he thought DeFries had oversold him). Ziggy was killed off in July 1973, replaced with a series of self-consciously camp

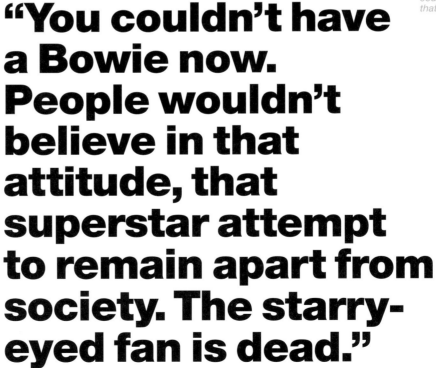

Simon Jordan of youth communications agency Magic Hat

"You couldn't have a Bowie now. People wouldn't believe in that attitude, that superstar attempt to remain apart from society. The starry-eyed fan is dead."

personae, from the Thin White Duke to the Pierrot of 'Ashes To Ashes' in 1980. But the Ziggy flash remains almost iconic, certainly the key image of Bowie, despite his many subsequent reinventions.

Three years after Ziggy said farewell, punk made its assault on the performer hauteur of the glam movement and attempted to make street culture, its dress and music, gritty and working class again. Being so strongly concerned with sex and identity – the Pistols would cover The New York Dolls' 'Personality Crisis,' re-working the idea in their own 'I Wanna Be Me', while X-Ray Spex managed a minor hit single with 'Identity' and The Clash thundered 'What's My Name' – excessive feminine make-up for boys became a norm. Patti Smith scorned make-up of any kind, while Annie Lennox began the development of her androgynous look and Siouxsie Sioux created the heavy Goth look that proved so popular during the Eighties. Punk's embracing of the perverse and promotion of a freak scene proved a valuable platform for genuinely gender-confused individuals, as well as confused teens. Wayne (later Jayne) County was the most public and successful transsexual singer of that time, widely accepted at punk gigs across the country, attracting scores of drag queens and brave boys who wanted to shock.

Punk wielded images to shock – a fact some would come to regret (pictured middle, Siouxsie Sioux)

Punk's promotion of cross-dressing in public helped the flowering of the New Romantic scene which followed it into the living rooms and discos of suburbia. Theatricality in general returned to the music scene, most notably when Stuart Goddard, then singer with a student group called The B-Sides, asked ex-Pistols manager Malcolm McLaren to be their manager. The self-styled svengali agreed and for a £1,000 fee told Goddard to put on a costume styled somewhere between Long John Silver and Sitting Bull and mark a white stripe across his cheeks and the bridge of his nose. Adam Ant was born. Two weeks later McLaren declared that Ant was too old and couldn't dance and left with the rest of the band to form Bow Wow Wow. Ant went on to be an Eighties phenomenon,

Vivienne Westwood

"I had known Adam [Ant] for some time as someone who used to hang around SEX, our boutique in the King's Road. I thought him a nice boy, very polite. Adam had been pestering Malcolm for ages to manage him. Eventually Malcolm gave him advice about stage presentation, like painting a big white stripe on his nose. He charged Adam £1,000 for that advice. That was probably the best advice Adam ever got."

Adam Ant's trademark tribal marking

shaping the New Romantic movement along with early Spandau Ballet and Duran Duran, when make-up on men became more widely acceptable. Adam Ant's look was like no other; as fresh as the new Burundi-beat driven sound that could only be categorised as Antmusic. Antfans everywhere Tippexed in their stripe and braved mockery from a giggling public.

After scoring a big hit with 'Fade To Grey', club organiser Steve Strange, the co-founder of Billy's Club, home of the original New Romantics, got to the stage where he would never leave the house without his make-up. Since he wore a lot, it must have taken a while to get a pint of milk. Boy George, of course, finally made cross-dressing respectable when he was allowed easy access to the living rooms across the globe via TV by singing his soul-derived ditties as lead singer of Culture Club. New Romanticism seemed to be all about men in make-up, of similar pancake measure to that worn by the original Dandies of the eighteenth century. Indeed, many New Romantic bands' videos featured a Georgian Dandy or two. Some New Romantic acts took themselves more seriously than others. Steve Strange and Dead Or Alive's Pete Burns both felt that they were performance artists in the mould of Bowie (who was to prove an enormous influence of the whole movement).

Make-up and a pseudo-fictional stage persona (often one adopted by the singers with almost method actor dedication) seemed to go hand in hand. Both Bowie and Goddard were the result of art school educations and became the types for whom concept albums were a given (Kraftwerk's identity, too, was shaped in 1973 by an art student, political activist and electric violin player, one Emil Schult). They were performers and make-up was an emphasis of their other-worldliness.

But they were not the only acts to realise the potential for make-up to challenge staid notions, to make a statement. Mod acts echoed the Mod delight in wearing eye-liner and mascara, with even

Kate Bush opted for glamour girl looks, all pout and soft focus – the gypsy-inspired look suited the theatricality of much of her music

The Real McCoy – London New Romantics

The Who's Roger Daltrey donning some eye liner. The Rolling Stones' Brian Jones and Mick Jagger more than dabbled with a bit of lippy (Marianne Faithfull famously modelled white lipstick). In the Seventies, Lou Reed wore heavy mascara in concert and on the cover of the blatantly-titled *Transformer* to provide the haven't-slept-for-a-month black bags under the eyes on the front, while completely changing gender on the reverse. Madonna contrasted the irony of 'Like A Virgin' with the most trampy of overdone make-up; a smudged, just-been-crying style of make-up application later worn by Courtney Love and her husband Kurt Cobain.

But you have to stay in the Seventies to find the most striking effect of rock cosmetics. Looking like a cross between characters from Star Trek and the cast of Cats, Kiss took a heavy, full-face white foundation and applied black panda eyes, whiskers and incredibly elaborate eye make-up. It's a look

Lou Reed's *Transformer* – the sickly, tired look of his kohl-eyes played on his association with drug experimentation

Robert Smith of The Cure, long-time exponent of Goth and well-known for his attachment to red lipstick, always applied slightly skewed

that made the band famous and ensured a loyal hard-core fan-base (somewhat less successful with its own make-up) which meant that Kiss dolls were being made as late as the end of the Nineties. Yet it also seemingly over-shadowed the band's 24-odd albums.

The make-up also gave the band an almost parodic mystique and both enhanced and contrasted their rock 'n' rolling faux-macho posturing. As with Bowie and Ant, there was the touch of clever marketing about their faces. Kiss was the brainchild of Gene Simmons, a former elementary school teacher and bass player, and

Pete Burns of Dead Or Alive and Morrissey. Despite wildly differing dress and musical tastes, neither was shy of enhancing with lipstick or eye-liner. Make-up's use by Morrissey was particularly striking against his 1950s Americana, neo-Rockabilly dress – an affordable look that was to become popular with students

Marilyn Manson – the only rock star since Bowie to use make-up quite so defiantly

Feel Mighty Real's Sylvester in the typical heavy eye-shadow of the 1970s

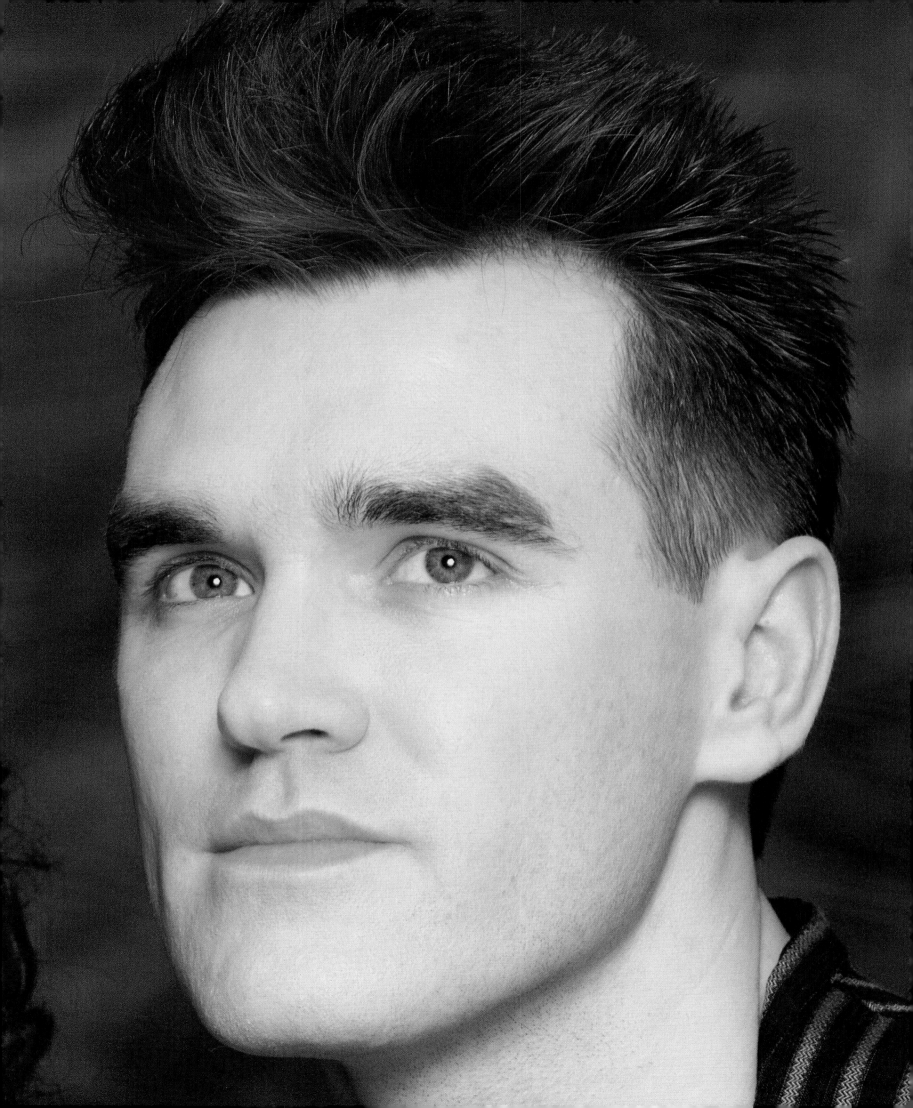

singer-guitarist Paul Stanley, who were bandmates in a Manhattan-based group called Wicked Lester. The pair had a concept for their new band right from the start, which was to perform in full theatrical regalia, including the white pancake make-up and elaborate facial markings, platform boots, and outrageous black and silver get-ups. Fully costumed, each member of the band was in effect a cartoon character: Simmons was the Bat Lizard, drummer Peter Criss was the Cat, guitarist Ace Frehley was the Spaceman, and Stanley was the Star Child. Inspired by such strong looks, Marvel Comics even published a Kiss comic book while the band, with albums titles like *Unmasked*, toyed with the notion that nobody knew what they looked like without their cosmetics. Indeed, when the band first showed themselves for who they were, on the cover of 1983's *Lick It Up*, Samson-like, they lost much of their appeal.

The New York Dolls and Iggy Pop kept theirs in place and possibly because they failed to sell as many singles or albums as Kiss and others, were a critical success. Alice Cooper, however, suffered critically from an excess of mascara and lipstick. His Halloween fright-style make-up, combined with a habit of wearing a live snake on stage as he beheaded baby dolls, meant that the great rock songs he wrote and performed – 'Under My Wheels', 'School's Out' and 'Elected' among them – were ignored by 'serious' music fans. Cooper proved a precursor to the Eighties more day-to-day ghoulishness that was Goth. Goths readily emulated the likes of Siouxsie Sioux and Robert Smith of The Cure by wearing shapeless black sweaters, violently back-coming their hair and finally adding a pack of powder and a slash of red lipstick (notably Reddest by Jane, Smith's lipstick brand of choice), seemingly applied blindfold. The funereal dress code and deathly

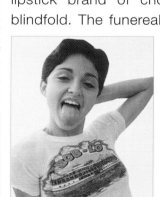

pallor adopted by teens who spent too much time alone in their bedrooms suited the band's songs of despair and dislocation.

The Nineties rather left the dressing table at home and opted for the barber shop. While so-called heroin chic made a showing towards the end of the decade – a pale and glassy-eyed look which moved from Calvin Klein catwalk to Garbage and Nirvana and ads for Packard-Bell computers (which was condemned in 1997 by no less a figure than U.S. President Clinton) – the decade brought more of an appreciation for the beard than make-up. Face furniture has not had a happy rock history. Consider Midge Ure in the Eighties, the Hitler 'tache of Sparks, the disco gay parody of the Village People biker, Frank Zappa's goatee and sideburns or George Michael's 'outed' beard and moustache. Only The Beatles sudden outgrowth of beards from 1968 – the point at which they ceased to be a working unit – passed muster. Facial hair in the Nineties, like the silly chin tufts of Kurt Cobain and Michael Stipe, has been more about personal statement – perhaps personal hygiene – than it has been about rock stars making fashion.

Perhaps only one rocker shaved and stayed true to the cosmetics testers. Marilyn Manson mixed Boy George with a pale imitation (literally as well as metaphorically) of Alice Cooper. But the world had moved on. Marilyn didn't gain any imitators. He was but an eye-shadow of rock's former painted glory.

The perennially bleary-eyed Alice Cooper. His and Kiss' use of make-up complemented glam rock's mix of biker and 1970s glam dress styles, as well as serving to undercut glam rock and heavy metal's often overt sense of masculinity

Kiss in all their painted glory

accessories

George
Michael's star
quality remains
hidden behind
sunglasses –
the rock star's
disguise

George
Michael's star
quality remains
hidden behind
sunglasses –
the rock star's
disguise

*Elvis made the big
spangly belt a
show piece – in
later years it would
also provide
support for his
expanding gut*

Rock 'n' roll, being the sound of a new, young generation who had previously gone straight from dressing like Mummy and Daddy for fun to dressing like them for work, had to have a childish streak. It's only natural, we all go through it. Newly-formed adolescents switch from carrying a teddy bear to bed to wearing that certain, single item which makes them stand out from the crowd, that item which offers the same degree of comfort as Teddy had, while also announcing to the world that here was someone special.

It is a little-known fact that, mellifluous voice though he had, nobody has ever been able to confirm if Roy Orbison had any eyes. He was always hidden behind a deep-space pair of sunglasses, as dark as his hair was pitch black, and the emotion in many of Orbison's performances was lost because the audience couldn't see his eyes. Not that he was alone. Even if Orbison did take sunglasses to excess, they have been part of the rock wardrobe since they were associated with being cool: from Ray Charles and Stevie Wonder (for more justified, less image-conscious reasons), right up to Nineties rap groups, dark glasses have been the quintessential rock star accessory.

Yet, generally, in the technicolour spectrum that is rock music's love of and influence over fashion, the accessory is out on the periphery, rarely recognised, seldom copied – and often with very good reason – by Joe or Josephine Public and, at first thought, of little consequence. It is only those fans so bent on being connected to their chosen idol – and by dint of the small but crucially individual accessory item they wear inspired by that idol – who know what little things make a difference. Elvis is most often remembered either in his GI uniform or white sequinned flared jump-suits. Few fans at

Facing page:
*Roy Orbison in his
signature glasses –
and a rare glimpse
of his eyes*

first knew or much cared what watch or belt he had on, for they were not items in his wardrobe that played a role in defining Elvis for his general public. However, the true obsessives, the real show-offs, knew exactly what they were and how to wear them.

With the explosion of rock 'n' roll as a mass market commodity, emerging performers (or their managers) soon realised that an item of clothing worn as a gimmick could work wonders in the recognition stakes. Such gimmicks had long-term relevance – these are the items donned by quick-change impersonators, a visual shorthand – working almost subliminally on the audience, as a metaphor for the performer or a particular song, an association that might be in defiance of the facts but nevertheless shapes the audience's perception of that performer. As well as dark glasses, thick-rimmed spectacles did the job for ordinary-looking Buddy Holly. Shadows guitarist Hank Marvin adopted his horn-rimmed specs in honour to Holly and became forever associated with them, and the inordinately simple Shadows step dance which he and the band would perform behind Cliff Richard as the born-again mild rocker sang 'The Young Ones'. Elvis Costello also adopted the nerd specs look, although it is uncertain whether it was in honour of Hank or Buddy. Johnny Kidd wore an eyepatch to belt out 'Shaking All Over' (in fact, he adopted his moniker and re-named his backing group The Pirates in order to really capitalise on the gimmick).

The cape has proven an infallible accessory for a range of artists, beginning with James Brown, who would have one draped over his shoulders as he kneeled, a quivering mess of emotion at the end of each gig, being comforted by a butler who would half-help the Soul Godfather off the stage,

Elvis imitated, but only the Godfather of Soul, James Brown, could wear a cape with such panache

"As for the word 'rock' – what does it mean today? It was not, as Don Maclean would have it, Buddy Holly's death that marked the day the music died. Holly had, in fact, broken with real rock before he croaked his last lyric. He was on the gravy train to Sugar Land already. So was Eddie. He quit the twenty flight climb and took the three gentle steps to heaven – wah-wah-ooh! Buddy and Eddie were saved by the grim reaper from building a legacy of saccharine trash that sticks like bubble-gum to the gates of Graceland."

Jack Good

Forever associated with nerdish looks, Buddy Holly's horn-rims made a bland boy memorable

only for James to dash back on for one more encore before collapsing again and in need of the cape. After James, the cape would drape many a distinguished and not-so shoulder, from Screaming Jay Hawkins to Screaming Lord Sutch (who nicked Hawkins' hokey Voodoo gimmick), and from Elvis to Rick Wakeman.

Colours themselves have become handy marketing tools for smart rock stars. Alvin Stardust finally made the pop charts after three attempts by wearing a black leather catsuit, black gloves and black quiff. He also wore massive fake-diamond rings over his black gloves. Prince to many means 'Purple Rain', his first hit release in the UK and, in the mind's eye, perhaps because of a clash between the song's title and his love of garish outfits, for many he is imagined at this time in one of his characteristic tight-fit suits, in purple. Yet this is a garment Prince didn't wear until he entered his New Power Generation phase.

Yet such aspects of dress – a particular colour, a particular hat – build strong associations. Short of being trademarked, they are, nevertheless, sophisticated marketing ploys. How do you make one rather ordinary looking pianist stand out from another ordinary looking pianist? You put him in wacky spectacles and change those spectacles on a daily basis. This myopic pianists gets a reputation, a long-term slot in the audience's mental slide-show of rock images. This is in part why everyone knows what Elton John

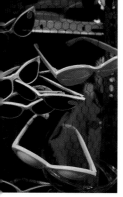

looks like. And not Billy Joel. And, in the Seventies, at the height of Glam, when John adopted his new frames of reference, it took something spectacularly outrageous to stand out. Thus Rick Wakeman (and Brian Eno) donning capes, Marc Bolan a top hat, Bowie an eye-patch (definitely a Johnny Kidd fan) – that's how silly it all got. But Elton is still wearing them over two decades later. Such attributes are often potent symbols. Perhaps this is why, unlike hairstyles, even types of dress, such motifs of individuality are rarely copied by subsequent generations of rock stars.

Indeed, accessories may make only the most slight appearance in a performer's career to have huge impact – something stylists, around since Epstein remodelled The Beatles but now a full-time profession with title for any serious boy band (if that is not a contradiction in terms), know instinctively. In 1984 an American three-piece electro funk band called Cameo – at the time relatively unknown outside of the US – lip-synched their way through their single 'Word Up' on the UK's six million-rated national television show *Top Of The Pops*. One of the band prodded enthusiastically at his synthesiser, another slapped his bass guitar with no less vigour. It was your averagely energetic performance, proceeded by many, followed by others.

And yet, next day, in school playgrounds, sixth-form colleges, universities, even factories and offices – in short, anywhere where *Top Of The Pops* was still a must-see programme – Cameo's performance was the only talking point. Why? Because, while flash dressing was nothing unusual during this New Romantic time, Larry Blackmon, Cameo's singer, went one step beyond. Underneath his Village People gay construction worker moustache, and way beneath his enormous flat-top conk of a hairdo, Larry was wearing a large, pillar-box red cod-piece. Now this Jean-Paul Gaultier creation wasn't something that was emulated by anybody. But everybody noticed it. It was the only time that Larry was to wear the item, but, as long as Cameo are remembered, Larry will be thought of in this industrial-strength posing-pouch.

The same effect was created – again using Gaultier paraphernalia – by Madonna, who commissioned the designer to create her stage outfits for her 'Like A Prayer' tour (in 1989). She was

From ski to you – hats and The Beatles

Larry Blackmon of Cameo, drawing attention to one particular part of his rock star anatomy with a Jean-Paul Gaultier designed codpiece

The Village People took the 1970s gay biker look and parodied it – the leather cap alone became a widely understood visual reference

"Bands have become mediums in their own right, a means for advertising brands. Brands need brand ambassadors to create the right impression for them. And as a brand the easiest way to build sales is to start with the right brand ambassador. But the brand and the person wearing it still have to have cultural authenticity. Their ilk probably have to already be wearing the brand or that particular look anyway. It's not as simple as putting a product on a star and expecting it to work."

Simon Jordan of youth communications agency Magic Hat

Madonna has been credited with popularising layered jewellery, crucifixes and the 'underwear as outerwear' fashion phenomenon. But the Jean-Paul Gaultier - designed conical bra (itself inspired by British street fashion and Vivienne Westwood) pointed in the right direction: rock star fashion as front-page news

Elvis quiff meets Bondian dinner suit and bow-tie – Bryan Ferry as the ultimate modern lounge room crooner

A glitzier, less sophisticated bow-tie for Michael Jackson – perhaps the glitter on his tie and waistcoat prefigures his famous sequinned glove

already widely associated with the trash chic of *Desperately Seeking Susan*, notably the lace gloves of her 'Like A Virgin' period, but Gaultier eclipsed these – both metaphorically and literally – with the conical bra, a garment which summed up the pop floozy's flaunt-it frock tactics all too well.

Others, too, have realised the power of the accessory. But Michael Jackson has been the one to work with it, to use such symbols in logos on record covers and gig merchandise, even long after the item has ceased to be worn. Apart from his button nose, two distinct accessories stand out for Jackson, both originating in his video for 'Billie Jean' – a song released in the UK in 1983, again suggesting that these visual cues are formed in the early part of an artist's career or a new phase in it. Similarly, John Lennon's association with round glasses marked the beginning of his solo career and was suggestive both of a fresh, ironically less image-conscious, seriousness and his new-found hippy philosophies.

Michael Jackson in the video for 'Billie Jean', launching his inspired short trousers and white socks look; a Jackson trademark, both literally and figuratively

The bow-tie works, the bow-tie stays, even with a cricket sweater – for Bryan Ferry, identifying marks were not to be given up lightly

The first accessory for Jackson was the fedora, which at one high moment in the 'Billie Jean' video is artfully spun out of shot. The fedora has made many return trips for Jackson – in press photographs but also creeping back some years later in the video for 'Smooth Criminal'. Such is the recognition of this hat – and its removal – that when Jackson performed 'Billie Jean' at the MTV Awards some 15 years after the song's release, the audience was palpably sitting in anticipation of the moment when he would spin his hat out to their seats. One could go so far as to

say that the hat for Jackson is a metaphor for his public and private lives, the latter of which he has fought a losing battle to maintain, even using his songs to comment on the situation. Jackson hides behind his hat, and its removal is the cue for the performer rather than the private man, to emerge.

But there is another item in the plastic one's wardrobe of greater significance still: the last thing one might imagine would make an effective corporate insignia for Jacksonworld. While his single sequinned glove made several appearances (later shelved in favour of something just as odd – white plasters wrapped around random fingers), an item lower down the pecking order of attractive garments became the big motif: his white socks. Again, although they were first revealed on the cover of his first solo album *Off The Wall* (1979), it was the 'Billie Jean' video that first decided their impact. In the video, Jackson hoists up his drainpipe trousers, revealing this flash of pale sock between hem and penny loafer, in order to strut his stuff – now-archetypal Jacksonesque dance movements involving either one shoe being stuck out and swivelled from side to side on the ball of the foot, or leaping knock-kneed up on to both toes. This sock style was a knowing nod to the groups he'd grown up with; watching the legendary Motown singing groups The Temptations and

Four Tops in the mid-Sixties, one cannot fail but be impressed with their choreographed dance steps, themselves highlighted by these flashes of sock between trouser and loafer.

The style was copied by soul fans around the world during the Sixties and early Seventies, with Northern Soul fans in the UK exaggerating the effect by wearing extremely baggy flared trousers at mid-calf in order to emphasise the footwork which, when lit by the reflective white socks, was unmissable. At the time Jackson was wearing his white socks prominently it was the height of Casual street fashion in the UK, the movement having grown out of the Soul Boy cult of the late Seventies (one personified by wedge haircuts, Hawaiian shirts and plastic sandals worn with, naturally, white socks) and was still worn by street-hustlers and minor wise guys in the US. They were still being worn by the moonwalking Jackson long after 'Billie Jean'. A logo incorporating the white socks and the latter dance movement even became used to represent MJJ Productions in merchandising opportunities. It said MJ, King of Pop Socks, without having to spell it out.

Other rock and pop acts have not been so astute in their use of the accessory and its symbolism. At times it has backfired: The Beastie Boys, now widely regarded as credible

The Temptations, all cropped trousers, silk socks and silkier voices

The Rolling Stones' Andy Warhol-designed cover for Sticky Fingers, with a hefty belt buckle and working zip-fly

alternative musos, are still strongly associated with their early, vapid snotty teenager look, comprising reversed baseball caps and necklaces bearing borrowed VW badges. The image has been so strong as to bar their Nineties music from a potentially larger audience.

The history of rock has also seen many accessories which are neither attractive nor effective marketing tools: for every Jimi Hendrix bandana, ever the symbol of biker cool and excess, there is the case of The Monkees' Mike Nesmith. He stood out painfully from the prototype boy band because of his ugly beanie hat – practically a statement of not wishing to get too involved in the image game, and one perhaps reflected in his reluctance to get involved in a Monkees revival tour in the late Nineties (though he did, in the end).

During the strange days of Glam in the early Seventies there were a number of gimmicks worn by rock stars which were invariably copied by rabid fans – Noddy Holder of Slade's mirrored top hat, for

The early Beastie Boys in some heavy metal – the look, itself a parady of rap uniform, was widely copied, with VW inundated with requests from car owners for replacement badges

Tommy Hilfiger

"The sense of style that rappers exhibited was terrific... the Beastie Boys wearing Volkswagen hood ornaments..."

"I suppose The Beatles were the biggest influence ever. Lennon, with his cap and leathers from us at Bazaar. And the Mary Quant mini skirt was made a hit in Europe and America and Japan by the Beatle girlfriends, Patty and Jenny Boyd. They all used to come to our studio to buy and were friends."

Mary Quant

instance – but none ever had a significant impact on fashion. Even Elvis' Seventies penchant for white silk scarves failed to ignite a boom of sales among middle-aged men facing a crisis. For a brief period in the early Eighties, Morrissey sparked a run on gladioli at florists wherever The Smiths were performing, but Levi's resisted the temptation to sell 501s complete with flowers in back pocket.

By the middle of the Nineties, accessories were not so unusual on the stage that they caused

any kind of fuss. Tattoos and piercings had become commonplace among both the performers and their admirers.

As the twentieth century comes to a close, the people standing under the stage are often as accessorized (pierced and tatooed), if not more so, than the people standing on the stage. Which is a mirror-shaded reflection of there being nothing new to be commandeered as an unusual and therefor identifying accessory in the world anymore. These days, the adults are dressing down, trying to be just like their kids.

Facing page
and far left:
*Morrissey went
beyong simple
clothing to find a
more fragrant
accessory –
bunches of gladioli.*

"Sports fashion was blessed by kids yearning to look like their favourite athlete. Now it's part of the vocabulary of casual style and an element of the rock and roll and hip-hop wardrobe for stars and fans alike."

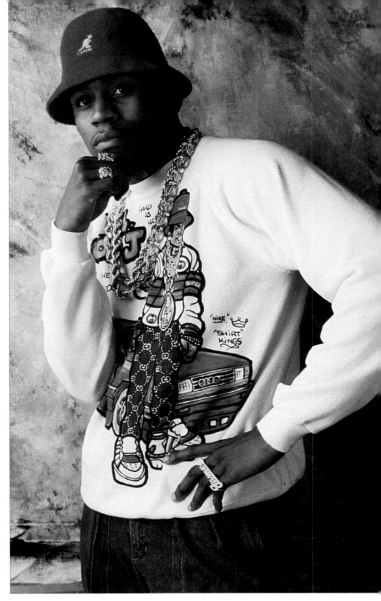

LL Cool J was at the forefront of hip-hop's appropriation of sportswear, seen here with his trademark Kangol fishing hat

Run DMC, among the founding fathers of hip-hop and also of many fashion accessories, notably the hats, the gold chains, as well the track-suits and Adidas sneakers – a look described by the youth style magazines in the early 1990s as 'old skool'

Public Enemy's B Boy styling epitomised the black militant look – berets, army boots, NATO Arctic camouflage kit and their own cross-wires logo, first seen on the cover of their 1987 debut album Yo! Bum Rush The Show. But the clock pendant always stood out